INKWELL

Spring 2020 • No. 35

INKWELL

MANHATTANVILLE COLLEGE
MFA in Creative Writing

Purchase, New York
No. 35 • Spring 2020

Editor:
Lori Soderlind

Managing Editor:
Donna Miele

Editorial Board:
David Albano, Sean Griffin, Alastair Murdoch,
Laurel Peterson

Manhattanville MFA Faculty:
Jeff Bens, Mark Nowak, Lori Soderlind

House Puppy:
Graci

Graphic Designer:
Danielle Cruz

Cover Art:
Parva Avis, Photograph
Danielle Wirsansky

Inkwell Journal 35

© 2020 Manhattanville College

ISBN: 978-1-7344369-0-7

Published in the United States by the Manhattanville College MFA Program, 2900 Purchase St., Purchase, NY 10577

inkwelljournal@gmail.com

Inkwell Journal, a literary journal published through the MFA program at Manhattanville College, seeks submissions in English of poetry, fiction, creative nonfiction/memoir, graphic novel/memoir excerpts, visual art, and genre-blurring work, as well as translations. We are interested in both established and new voices, including voices that have been historically under represented.

For full submission guidelines and to purchase the current issue, visit inkwelljournal.submittable.com

CONTENTS

FICTION

NONFICTION

SPECIAL SECTION: SANCTUARY

POETRY

FICTION

NONFICTION

EDITOR'S NOTE

In planning this issue of *Inkwell Journal*, we editors were looking for a timely and relevant subject to feature as a special section. We wanted a topic that could be interpreted both politically—inviting commentary on this strange reality TV show that has preempted our regular lives—and broadly, inviting work that reflects the nature of our times wherever it shows up.

What topic might bring us art on the pulse of this era with all its division and isolation, its race-baiting and dog-whistling, its border closings, its climate crises, its violence and ignorance, its rising white supremacy and threatening autocracy, and its too-common failures of human decency, sometimes writ large?

Sanctuary. Isn't this what we want?

But if it was comfort we sought, our special section does not let us off so easily. The writers who answered our call for writing about "Sanctuary" reveal that a "lack thereof" is what now preoccupies the group mind. What I expected when I began reading submissions was an avalanche of writing on immigration issues, with a few broader interpretations suggesting safe harbors in difficult times. Instead we received only a slim few works addressing refugees and immigration; the avalanche was of work suggesting that very little sanctuary exists anywhere in the world, today.

That is indeed art offering us an honest reflection of ourselves. And perhaps it has always been this way. The struggle is real and really is with us, always; it is part of art's work to confront the pain and violence of our time, whatever time that may be, and to raise our voices above it without pretending that the pain and violence and the fear can be neatly avoided. We can't stick our collective head in the sand. Unless of course you are actually a turtle, as is the hero in an essay that ends this volume.

This issue of *Inkwell Journal*, then, offers you a section on "Sanctuary" where you will find spiders, grief, failed love, burning libraries, shifting identities, loss, violence, and more. It's sometimes rough. If there is comfort to be found in it, the comfort is the work itself. Its existence. The creativity and vision and craft in these bursts of prose and poetry demonstrate that the spark does not extinguish in the dark; when we read we find ourselves dissolving more deeply into genuine connection with others, which, come to think of it, is the most enduring safe place I can think of. Sanctuary.

The rest of the issue is not themed but equally invites you to step beyond "the times" and into that timeless sanctuary of reading and creativity. I wish for you the experience of reading this journal straight through, as a book. Give it an hour or two, on a couch, with a warm beverage and maybe a dog at your side. That's how I experienced it, in the darkest winter days of late 2019, as strange a time as any to be alive, I suppose. And yet, a bit of joy in this effort. Quite a bit of comfort to hear these voices, and know that our struggles are real and our art is, too.

Lori Soderlind, Director
Manhattanville College MFA Creative Writing Program
December 2019

KATHERINE FLANNERY DERING
HERONS

It's March, and the herons are back near the Post Inn.
The sky above the forest of swamped, dead trees
is alive with looping wings. Great straw nests top barren
branches, the trees flooded by beavers downstream.
I watch with my binoculars in the chill breeze as high
in the ghost trees, thirty feet above the still-frozen field,
nesting pairs tend to their castles of sticks, caring
for their chicks through raging storms this frigid spring.
O, how many of us could use a lesson in fidelity!
The temperature drops. The trees complain with freezing
cracks.
This world can be a hostile place. But for now, the ash trees
are aglow, each branch highlighted with a thin layer of snow,
a play of light and dark, solid and ethereal,
the future filled with possibilities.

MARCESCENCE

Dear Kay,
Late fall afternoons grow dear to me, and I think
of you, our afternoons in the garden swing.
I love the strips of sun struggling past tree trunks,
the different textures of their bark—oak,
maple, ash—sturdy caches of sap, harbingers

of future life. But is this any comfort
to the great aunt we never knew
who died of the Great Flu? Or to me and you?
Downed oak leaves dance in sudden wind eddies,
while the beech trees seem unwilling to succumb

to the barrenness of winter. Does the leaf that falls
think of next year's replacement? I think not.
Did you know, some trees hold on to their leaves
all winter? The sun slips below the horizon.
We still have weeks before snow.

Morgan Eklund

Three Short Fragments About Things in The Wrong Places

I

Ice on the Beach

I have finished another apology.
I am all the endings—or the never-beginnings.

Is it possible that I started as a ghost or
a single stem in the sea?
Or as winter on a beach?
Ice never seems to belong there—
crystalizing into sand.

II

Bug in the Theatre

I have finished another apology.
I feel I am always in rehearsal—

waiting for my birth.
A bug attacking the spotlight, one hit. Another.
It hasn't decided. Is it the bug? Is it the light?
Is it something beyond the light?

III

Moon in the Factory

I have finished another apology.
I want to be the moon
because it doesn't apologize
when it's broken—a crescent—

There's a factory full
of more moons.
Carving another
and another
it never tires.
Our temporary, endless pull.

CHRISTY BAILES

IDÉE FIXE

My senescent dad picks up sticks
in a plaid dressing gown
and talks like a baby to Tuxy,
who trails behind his shuffling steps.
Cat talk, he calls it.

When he runs out of sticks,
              he climbs the extension ladder
              with fearless feebleness by
              stepping around rungs and onto the roof
              to push pine needles off the ledge.
He waves and grins,
terrifying neighbors,
who yell, *Get down from there!*

Mom's a nervous wreck,
              poking her head out
              each hour
              like a cuckoo,
              checking on her doddering groom,
but she always goes back to
              decorating some holiday with more holiday.

Like always, he escapes the roof
and enters the junk jungle,
              pushing his paunch
              through whatever time of year
happens to be inside the house,
              passing remote shelves
of pressed glass, cut glass, carnival glass, milk glass,
              cranberry glass, and depression glass;
but he doesn't see *his* stranded antiques,
              he sees

mom's jewelry hanging
            like crows' meat
      in the crowded hallway
            as he moves through
      humming fluorescents.

Having heard dad's dynamic door slam, mom knows he's off
the roof.
            She opens the door to my old bedroom
                        and squeezes through boxes stacked to the
ceiling
            to look for
                  a decorative decoy
                        decaying in the dangerous
                        entrapment of her lost childhood.

While mom digs, dad finally makes it to the bathroom.
      He powders himself
                  and everything else
with talcum powder from London,
            then scoots and arranges and replaces
                        thrift store stuff
                        with other
thrift store stuff,
            which is stuffed in every drawer.

Near the end of his daily ritual,
he admires his hypotactic décor
            from a commode's view
                  with a Marilyn Monroe clock on the right
an Aristotle sculpture on the left
                  and a small wooden Jesus behind
                  to absolve
                  their festive mess.

MĒARA LEVEZOW

BIG GAME

I remember the disorderly ecosystem
of family card games: crouching
beneath an expansive canopy
of dining room table, waiting
for the fall of ceramic poker chips
like heavy tropical rain. I was an orchid

in the undergrowth, barefoot and flushed, face
flushed like *flush beats a straight*, straight
flush like a straight face like a *Queen
high bets*. Screeching aviary of adult laughter
and the energy of aunties in late night
like a swarm of insects. Only dappled light got through,

only jacks or better opens. I knelt near
the mangrove of Mom's legs and stalked
like the hunter, like the *deuces the jacks
and the man with the ax,* hoping to find
the chip with the smiley face inked in the center:
the good luck. The talisman.

Meara Levezow

Amelia Earhart Responds To a Recent Discovery

They found a jar of freckle cream today
on an island in the South Pacific
and immediately assumed it was mine,
as if feminine vanity outweighed
my years of training and my prolific
knowledge of aerodynamics: the bottom line
is any extra space is saved for fuel.
I always used to wear bloomers in school,
and once stole a pistol to shoot the gray
rats in my grandfather's barn. The trick
was that my female scent would undermine
their instincts. Watching their bodies explode in the hay,
I didn't mourn or find myself heartsick.
My only wish: to shoot a straighter line.

Shawn Rubenfeld
I Am Here

Jonah Etkin was going to Ukraine and he wouldn't let anyone, not even his grandmother, talk him out of it.

"Four thousand miles for a girl you've never met," his grandmother said, putting a carton of almond milk in her shopping cart, coughing into a fist. It was only the second time she had brought it up since Jonah got off the L train to meet her in Sheepshead Bay. A new record. "They *hate* the Jews there. They could kidnap you. Don't you remember my brothers? Steven and Sammy. They killed them."

"*They* didn't kill them," Jonah said. "The Nazis did. The Germans. Things are different now."

"Kids would spit on me when I went to school," she said. "They said *go home. We don't want you here.* Zhidovka, that's what they used to call me. Jew girl. Jewess. That was Russia. I lived there. I know."

Jonah wheeled the cart forward. One of the wheels was stuck, so he kicked it until it was spinning again. They were at the Belarus Supermarket, catty-corner from the gray towers of her apartment complex on Neptune Avenue. It was just before five, nearly rush hour. The irony of it all certainly wasn't lost on him.

"Did you hear me?" she said. "Why do you have to go on the Internet to find some Russian girl? Tell me what you're hoping to accomplish. I still don't understand."

In the beginning, he liked the attention. He liked telling people he was going to Ukraine because most people he knew hadn't been. What he didn't like was telling people *why* he was going. *Why not?* he would say, to which most people would look at him with pity, as if they knew. *Why not Paris or Rome or London?* they'd ask. *I'm a travel contrarian,* he'd tell them, shrugging. His grandmother was the only one who really knew *why*, like she was the only one who knew he had used Rogaine on the thinning spot at the back of his scalp, that he didn't have the guts to ask a girl out until he was twenty-eight, that she had given him a fake number. But that was all then. Now, he was leaving in the morning on a flight to Krakow, which was a mere train ride away from the Ukrainian border. A train ride away from Anja.

Jonah had been messaging her since February, which was when he learned about *RussianLove.com* from one of the salesmen at work. There was a nominal fee to join and another small translation fee for each message exchanged, but it was a small price to pay for a potential lifetime of companionship. Anja was a waitress at a restaurant in Lviv, Ukraine, the youngest of four daughters and the only one— at thirty-three—not yet married. Anja said she wanted to settle down and that she liked the pictures Jonah had sent, that in them he looked very "noble" and "American."

He told her that she looked very Russian.

Ukrainian, she wrote back.

Six months later, Anja suggested Jonah visit her in Lviv. Even then he thought it was crazy. Their conversations had been fun because they had been secret. It was also why they had been so easy. This was the thrill he had missed out on as a kid, a few short years before social media and instant messaging became a thing. He'd read her invitation, twisted the cap off a beer, and chugged it until he felt sick. Later, he opened a map and zoomed in on Lviv. He panned around the country, the region. He tried to remember the name of the town his grandmother was from. It was, he realized, closer to him than it seemed. The entire world was closer than it seemed. He checked flights on Expedia. He watched

YouTube videos about Ukraine. About Poland. He spent nights staring at pictures of Anja. The sad, hesitant look in her eyes. It was what made him fall in love with her in the first place, though he couldn't say why. Maybe because in them he could see himself. Or a part of him that was missing. In all her photos, she looked away from the camera, as if she were ashamed. As if she, too, had lost something.

He called his grandmother. He figured she, if anyone, would understand.

"You're doing *what?*" she said. "For a *Russian* girl? No thanks."

"Ukrainian," Jonah said.

She had paused briefly. "What the hell is the difference?" she said.

And that was how Jonah Etkin, thirty-five, insurance salesman from Union, New Jersey, ended up in Krakow. Four thousand miles away from home, yet he didn't feel any different. Tired, definitely, and with a cutting headache, but hungry and eager to make the most of his time here. Just one day from meeting Anja for real. One day from starting the rest of his life.

It was windy and raining, but the cobblestoned streets of Krakow's old town were pulsing with the energy of camera-wielding tourists. People appeared and disappeared. Some spoke English. Others were standing in front of stores waving passersby inside. "Out of the rain, out of the rain," they said. "Dry, dry inside." Jonah rolled his suitcase from one busy alley to another, devising a plan for the day. It would have to start with some self-care. Shower, shave, lotion. Then, maybe, he could wander around the market square and see some of the old town. He could visit the Wavel Castle or examine the wooden altarpiece of St. Mary's Basilica. He didn't pack a rain jacket, so he'd have to find one of those, too.

He rolled his suitcase through the swinging door of his hotel and dried his face with his hand. The red-haired woman behind the counter greeted him with a warm smile and asked for his passport.

She was scanning it and typing on her computer, and he was taking big gulps from a water bottle when she asked if he was interested in a ride to Auschwitz.

"Excuse me?" he said. "To where?"

"Nazi Concentration Camp," she said, as if she thought he had never heard of Auschwitz. "We provide a shuttle van free of charge. Round trip. Leaves in one hour."

The door opened behind him and let in the sounds from outside—winds whistling, horns honking, people laughing.

For the first time, it struck Jonah that he was in the kind of place where one could arrange a casual visit to Auschwitz at the front desk of a tourist-class hotel. His grandmother would have been mortified. He thought of the picture she had on her dining room table of her twin brothers, Steven and Sammy. Young and broad-backed. Their little sister standing between them, a valley shielded by mountains. Now: dead.

"Yes?" the woman at the desk said.

Why not? Jonah thought. *I'm here. I have time to kill. It would be interesting to see.*

One hour later, Jonah was sitting at the back of the hotel's shuttle van to Auschwitz, where he watched the green hills of southern Poland dancing on the other side of the wet window, where he read and re-read some of his messages from Anja.

I'm so excited to see you, he wrote. *Can't believe I'm finally on your side of the world.*

Auschwitz was comprised of two camps: Auschwitz I, the labor camp, and Auschwitz II, the death factory. Jonah couldn't remember if he knew this.

At Auschwitz I, where the van parked, Jonah split from the others and walked first around the camp's perimeter, following the double-layered electric fence. Inside the camp, tour groups passed one after another, the people herded along the displays in the barracks. The rain was coming down hard now, so visitors would run from one structure to the next as if their lives depended on it, shielding gigantic cameras with their coats.

Eventually, Jonah fell in step with them, moving through the exhibits slowly, taking photos of the guard towers, contemplating the display of shoes. He was struck by the enormity of it all. He was overwhelmed by the rain. He was filled with disgust. Still, he couldn't stop thinking about Anja. Anja walking there with him, sneering at all the tourists. Anja bending down to tie her shoes. Anja in her mother's house, doing her hair, thinking about him. Anja's big sad smile. Anja's soft cool hand.

On the toilet at the visitor's center, he loaded her profile on his phone. Nothing had changed. *Hello! My name is Anja and I am from Lviv in Ukraine. Lviv is a city in West Ukraine. I enjoy cooking and dancing and cake. I am looking for someone to share my life with. I want to explore the world. That is my dream.* He began typing another message to her about his day so far, though he knew she wouldn't read it until later that night after she was home from work. Some days, she said, her feet were so tired that all she could do was sit in the bath and soak with the bubbles. Once, she sent a photo of her toes covered with bubbles. Her toenails weren't painted. They were liberated toes. It made him love her even more.

After finishing the message, he swiped to a photo of her standing by a lake with her father and grandfather. All three were the same height. The men had their heads leaned slightly down, not smiling. Her grandfather's lips were raised, his cheeks were bunched up and covering his eyes. His shoulders were healthy and broad. He was a good looking man, didn't look a day past seventy, though simple math would make him at least eighty. Suddenly, Jonah wondered what side of history he had been on. Did he turn his head as his Jewish neighbors were massacred? Did he cheer on the murderers? Had he been a murderer himself? Or was he among the few who fought back?

Outside, Jonah walked past a row of souvenir stalls and food carts and decided that it didn't matter what Anja's grandfather did or didn't do. What mattered was who he was now. What mattered was that his granddaughter was just across the border in Lviv, and that Jonah was only one day away from meeting her. He bought a hot dog and settled into a dry picnic table, covered by a yellow and white umbrella. "Yes," he said, as if convincing himself. "Life goes on. Just look at my grandmother."

At the table behind him, an ice cream cone slipped from a child's hand. The girl laughed, seeming to wipe her hands clean of it. Then, she folded her arms across her chest and screamed bloody murder.

~

Three kilometers from Auschwitz I was Auschwitz II, Birkenau, the death factory, a sprawling complex that seemed to go on forever. At the very back of the site, far from the wandering tourists, were the remains of a barracks called Kanada, where the Nazis sorted and stored inmates' belongings. Like most of the camp, Kanada had been demolished on the Germans' retreat. All that was left now were foundations, which formed neat rectangles of wet soil.

Jonah walked around the buildings' footprints and peered down at the puddles of mud in the dirt. Chipped buttons were pressed into the ground, as if seeds germinating in the soil. Most of them were off-white and peeling. Some were broken in two. At first Jonah figured they were part of a memorial, maybe some kind of art installation. Then he read the sign nearby that said that inmates' belongings were still being recovered from this site, even today. Forks. Knives. Fabric. Buttons. Jonah stood looking at the buttons for a long time, wiping his forehead free of rain, blowing his nose into the rolls of toilet paper he had taken from the hotel bathroom. Finally, he pulled one of the buttons from the dirt and rubbed it clean. It was blue and brown, chipped in a corner. In better shape than most of the others. He twirled it between his fingers. It had two small button-holes like eyes forced open. He put it up to his nose. It didn't smell of death. It smelled of rain, of life. He could see Anja wearing it—pasted onto her blouse. He trapped it in a fist. He was lost in himself. He wanted to say something no one had ever heard. To hear something no one had ever said. But the only thing he returned to was Anja. Anja in Lviv. Anja at Auschwitz. Anja and this button. It had a gravity all its own. He dropped the button into his pocket and walked on.

He stayed at Birkenau until the guard towers were cloaked in a dark mist. Then he headed for the main gates, but was stopped when someone grabbed his shoulder.

"Your pocket," said a voice. It was a security guard.

Jonah pointed at himself. "Me?"

"You have something that isn't yours," the guard said. He pointed to a sign forbidding visitors from taking anything from the site.

"Oh," Jonah said, feeling around his pocket for the button. "I was just . . . I was only . . . You see, my uncles were . . ." He stopped. He couldn't find it.

The guard took Jonah into the office and forced him to empty his pockets onto a table. Toilet paper. Hotel room keys. Business card from the shuttle van driver. He checked his sneakers and socks, the lining of his shirt, even his hair—at least what was left of it. The button was gone.

The guard called over a second guard. They talked for a long time in Polish.

"You're lucky," the second guard said. "This is a serious crime."

"But I don't have anything," Jonah said.

"That's why you're lucky."

~

Pictures from Auschwitz lingered in Jonah's mind as he sat in the front seat of an Uber the next morning to catch the train to see Anja. They remained even as he told his driver that he was going to Ukraine, as the driver stopped the car in the middle of the road then and there, turned to face him, smiled, and said, "I am from Ukraine"; as he described Anja for this driver.

"I'm not sure why I came to Poland at all, actually," Jonah said. "Some of my family is from here but I don't know where exactly. It was long before I was born. Something like that brought me, I guess. Besides, the flight was cheap. That was it, to be honest. It was because the flight was cheap. I should have just gone to straight to Lviv. It's obvious I don't belong here."

And the driver said, "You know, Lviv for a long time was a Polish city. Some people here still think it's a Polish city, called Lwow. Ukraine politics are complicated like that."

"American politics, too," Jonah said.

The train ride was seven hours long, two of which were spent stopped as border agents charged through the train with dogs and guns. "What were you doing in Poland?" one of them asked. "Just visiting," he said. "Did you bring anything from Poland? Guns, cigarettes, animals?" He said no, not even a button.

"Where is your final destination in Ukraine?"

"Lviv."

"For what?"

"Tourism."

"Fine." The border agent stamped his passport and immediately he opened to the page. The ink was red and running dry.

The train coughed into the Lviv-Holovnyi railroad station twenty minutes early. Jonah collected his bags and walked up the steps to the main concourse, an open-air art nouveau structure with a steel dome and twin chandeliers. He cleaned his face in the bathroom and gave himself a quick pep talk. He rinsed his glasses in the sink. He blew his nose. Then, he found a cozy spot in the corner by the arrivals board where he could wait for Anja, where he could pull out his phone and look at photos of Anja, where he could still his racing heart by imagining their life together. He'd stay in this country if he had to, he decided. As long as they were together, nothing else mattered.

He waited for one hour, then two hours, but still couldn't will that photo of Anja to life. He tried again to will that photo to life. And again.

Finally, he messaged her. *I'm here,* he wrote. *By the Arrivals board.* After another hour he called *RussianLove.com* to explain that he was in Ukraine and was worried that recent notes had been translated incorrectly. They were to meet today in Lviv. That was the plan. That had always been the plan. They had even spoken of it yesterday. At least that was how he understood it. But now he was in Lviv and there was no Anja. And he knew she wouldn't stand him up like this. They promised to get back to him promptly, but never did. He stood shaking. He tried calling again but couldn't get through to anyone. A group of children circled him asking for change. He was ready to kick one of them but thought better of it.

Four hours. Five hours. His entire body ached. The battery on his phone was dying and there wasn't a power outlet in sight. So, he did the only thing he could think to do: walk the mile into Lviv, check into his hotel, and try on his own to find Anja.

Lviv, Jonah discovered, was Krakow's ugly cousin. Maybe he was just bitter. The words Anja so often used: dear, dearest, hugs and kisses. The pictures she sent of herself on a checkered blanket at the park, on a cracked wooden bench at the market square, sipping coffee on the stone steps of a courthouse. The money he spent every time a message was exchanged. The money he spent coming here to Lviv, where the cobblestone streets were shaded but dry, where little green buses packed with people puffed out a cloud of black smoke, where the women all looked like Anja. Long legs, blonde hair sometimes dyed black, dark eye shadow. They didn't smile at him when he walked by. Often they didn't look at him. And then there were the cars that stirred up mountains of dust. Dust that obstructed his view of the street and, as luck would have it, nearly ignited an asthma attack.

He spent the rest of the night trying to get through to *RussianLove.com*. He sent twelve messages to Anja. *I am here. I am here. I am here.* He read through their entire history, trying to figure out exactly where she worked.

His grandmother called to make sure he was okay. *Of all the places in the world, you go and pick Russia? Why? Why did you have to go there, Jonah? What's there that you can't find here? Tell me.*

He didn't sleep. The glowing light from his phone kept him up. Swipe on, swipe off. No messages. Anja's profile. *Hello! My name is Anja and I am from Lviv in Ukraine.* Her photos. Her face. His life. The rest of his life. Poof.

In the morning, he ventured into Lviv's city center. The town's heart was Rynok Square, whose anchor was a courthouse with a banner demanding that Ukrainian prisoners of the Kremlin be released. Tenement houses snaked around fountains with Greek sculptures, where groups sat and smoked. The blue and yellow Ukrainian flag waved from every rooftop. A tram passed every few minutes, often without warning, and the people walking in its path had to jump out of the way. Wooden carts were set up on the north side of the square with painted eggs for souvenirs. The sun was just now emerging from above the square's only black tenement, a building that looked as if it were made of charred sandstone. There was a light breeze and the scent of woodsmoke and meat, occasionally fused with coffee and exhaust smoke. He wondered: where would he and Anja be now? How much would they have already done together?

Without a lead, he walked into restaurants one by one and asked if there was an Anja who worked there. Many didn't understand what he was asking. Shoulders shrugged. Some of the restaurants were quite gimmicky. One was filled with gas lamps, another with thousands of upside-down postcards. When he said "Anja," the response was often "Food?" He would shake his head and show them pictures from his phone. The person he was speaking to would sometimes lean closer to look then pull back as if finally understanding and say something like, "Oh." Then they would shake their heads. Twice, upon hearing the name *Anja*, the host or hostess nodded and disappeared into a back room, then emerged with a woman who wasn't Anja. One even pointed at herself and said "me?" These moments were the hardest. He listened to the whir of the wind, masking the bells that rang in the distance. The beggars who played violin, cello. The people who formed circles around them and clapped.

An enormous hunger erupted from within him. He followed a crowd into the next restaurant, a cafeteria-style lunch hall called Gusya. The entryway had mock-columns and the walls were covered in orange and brown bathroom tiles. He slid a tray across a busy service line and pointed pathetically at a few things, not that he knew what any of it was. Tray full, he was ushered to the cashier, who punched numbers into a register and said flatly: "Forty-four hryvnia." He reached into his pocket and pulled out a fifty but she shook her head no.

He looked at the bill again. "What's wrong with it?" he asked. "You said forty-four?"

"Um," she said and looked to the other lane for help. The woman ringing there ignored her. "No English," she said, shrugging.

"Forty-four," he said, pointing to the register. "Fifty," he said, pointing to the bill. "Here."

She didn't say anything this time. She just stood there, scratching her face. People carrying trays of borscht and eggs and fried meatballs lined up behind him, some looking on.

Jonah was getting enraged. "Do you need smaller change?" he asked, fishing out three twenties. "This is is all I have. Here. Money. Sixty."

She didn't shake her head this time. She leaned back as if she were afraid of him. Desperate, Jonah held up his money for the people waiting in line.

"English?" he asked. "Forty-four. Fifty. Sixty." Oh, how he wished Anja were with him. He was sweating. He wanted to go home. This would be the end of it. He would go back to Poland tomorrow and leave this miserable place once and for all. His grandmother was right. Russia could have Lviv for all he cared.

Still the cashier stood there, looking uninterested. A few people started yelling in Ukrainian.

Finally a man with a tank-top and crewcut pushed forward and pointed to Jonah's pockets. Sweating, Jonah emptied them onto the counter. That was when he saw it there: the button. But how? He grabbed it and stuffed it back into his shorts.

The man shook his head, laughing. He struggled to find the word. "Change," he said, pointing out the window. "Bank."

"Why bank?" Jonah said. His arms were shaking. His body felt twice as heavy. He heard the blast of a horn and watched as a yellow bus pulled up to the window. "Twenty plus twenty plus twenty is sixty. What else do I need?"

"Exchange," said the man.

"Exchange what?"

The man looked down and then snapped his finger. He snatched one of the bills and held it up to Jonah's face. "Poland," he said, pointing to it. "Polish." Then he pointed to the ground. "Ukraine. *Greev-na.*"

Now it hit him. Jonah had forgotten to exchange his pocketful of Polish zlotys for Ukrainian hryvnia. He grabbed the bill from the man. *Naradowy Bank Polski.* The side-profile of King Kazimierz, a man who, fittingly enough, had been responsible for welcoming millions of European Jews into Poland. In fact, the Jewish district of Krakow, Kazimierz, was named in his honor.

"Sorry," he said to the cashier. "Do you take credit cards?" She shrugged and looked at the man with the crewcut. Jonah held out a credit card and pointed to it. She shook her head.

"No," the man with a crewcut said. "No card."

Jonah put his tray back and left.

Outside, he felt the button between his fingers. He held

it up to the sun and rubbed the place where it was chipped. He couldn't help but check the buttons on his own shirt. They were all there. And he was, too. Somewhere. Here or there. And so was Anja. In another restaurant, maybe. On this street, passing by, bells ringing like on a bicycle, disappearing like ash.

He felt he couldn't risk being seen with this stolen button and didn't want the responsibility of carrying it. Not alone, without Anja. Not here. He found a dry well beyond the market square and tossed it in.

With nothing better to do, he ordered chicken strips at KFC and went back to dipping into restaurants, asking for Anja. Restaurants located underground. Chocolate restaurants. Restaurants on rooftops, up winding flights of dark stairs. Fast-food restaurants. Pizza restaurants. The answers: *no, no, no, me?*

It was dusk when he happened upon the ruins of Lviv's Silver Stone Synagogue, well beyond the market square, where kids were playing and where parents were sitting on one of the memorial stones which explained in English how the synagogue had been destroyed by the Nazis during the war. What else was new? Everything that had once been Jewish in this part of the continent was destroyed during the war. He'd known it before landing in Krakow. The stone explained that Lviv was once a major center of Jewish culture, known in Yiddish as Lemberg and in Polish and Lwow. But what traces of that life were here now? Only this, it seemed. A small square where parents could feed their children sandwiches. Footprints of rotting stone. This and a chipped button that lay hidden at the bottom of a well, lost yet again.

As he turned to leave, he saw next to the ruins of this synagogue a cafe called the Silver Stone. The awning had the restaurant's name not only in Ukrainian and English but in Hebrew. He walked up to it. Lamps shaped like menorahs flanked the front door, which was closed. A Jewish restaurant. At least here were people like him. Maybe they could even advise him what to do next. They could all share a laugh. Another stupid American scammed. What a country.

He pulled on the front door but it was locked. He tried to look in a window but couldn't see anything. Just another relic of Jewish life here lost for good. He turned away. Then the door creaked open and a man with bright blonde hair in a yellow t-shirt and slacks called out in English.

"You came to eat?" he said. Jonah had never been happier to hear someone speak English.

"Are you open?"

"Yes, yes. Just now. Come in."

He did. Inside, the place was like a Jewish museum. The walls were filled with photos of Jews. Hundreds, even thousands of Jews. There were Haggadahs and framed photos of the Hebrew alphabet and pages from Jewish song books. Glittery Stars of David hung from the ceiling. If only my grandmother were here to see this, he thought, snapping a photo with his phone.

"Sit anywhere you'd like," the man said, smiling. "I'll get you a menu."

Jonah sat and let out a deep breath. He put his wallet on the table and flipped through it. He wanted to tell this man everything.

When the man returned, he was in costume: a too-big black top hat over his blonde hair and paste-on long-curled sidelocks like Orthodox payot.

"Shalom," he said, adjusting the sidelocks. "I am a Jew and welcome you to our Jewish restaurant. Here is your English menu. We serve Jewish food here. All kosher. Just so you know, we don't have prices on the menu because we barter." He folded his arms against his chest.

Jonah thought that maybe he had heard him wrong. He opened the menu and saw that there were no prices. "You what?" he said.

"We barter," the waiter said.

"What do you mean barter?"

"I mean this is a Jewish restaurant and Jews are good at bartering." There was a pause. "Don't you know anything about Jews?"

Jonah hoisted his head as if woken from a dream. "But are you actually Jewish?"

"I am," said the waiter, pulling on one of his fake curls.

"What's your last name?"

"Schwartz. My family are accountants. Why do you ask?"

"Do you know Hebrew?"

"Just a few words. Not all Jews know Hebrew, Jonah."

Jonah sat up. That was true. *He* didn't know Hebrew. All those years of Hebrew school had left him with nothing but a Hebrew name he couldn't remember.

"Wait," he said. "How do you know my name is Jonah?"

The waiter pointed at the wallet on the table, opened to the driver's license. "Etkin, Jonah," he said.

Jonah put the wallet back in his pocket.

The waiter held his hands to his face and stepped back. "Don't worry. We don't steal. Now what do you like to eat? If you're afraid to bargain I can tell you what to say when you order. We have prompt cards with lines you can use to make it easy. May I recommend a few dishes to begin with?"

The door to the restaurant opened and a young woman walked in.

"Shalom!" said the waiter. "Welcome to our Jewish restaurant."

The woman nodded at the waiter and sat at one of the

wooden barstools.

"Can I have a minute, please," Jonah said.

"A minute. Yes, of course. But remember, time is money."

"Where's the bathroom?"

"Just down there," the waiter said, pointing.

Jonah stood and walked to the bathroom. On the way he looked at the photos on the wall. Jews big and small. Jews happy and sad. Jews at school. Jews standing in groups on the street. In another world this might have been his life. He, Jonah Etkin, a Jew in Poland. A Jew in Ukraine. So many generations. So much left behind. Then, he saw something he couldn't explain, like that button at the bottom of the well, like whatever it was that got him on that van to Auschwitz. It was a photograph he had seen thousands of times before, the centerpiece of his grandmother's dining room. His dead uncles, Steven and Sammy. Except instead of posing with a little girl standing between them, here they stood alone. His grandmother, closing the space between them in the photograph Jonah knew by heart, was gone. Jonah closed his eyes and opened them again. This was impossible, of course. There was only one copy of this picture and it was with his grandmother in Brooklyn. Sweating, he ripped the photo the wall and brought it to the waiter, who was leaning against the bar, twirling his paste-on Jew curls.

"Where did you get these photos?" he asked.

"These are of friends," the waiter said.

"These are my uncles."

"Impossible," the waiter said. "These are *my* uncles. Also, this photo was taken a hundred years ago. And you don't look very old. Not as old as me." Then, "Wait. Are you a Jew like us? I can give you a discount. We look after each other. It's how we're all so successful, we yids. That isn't a derogatory word, you know. Yids. Don't listen to what they tell you. In fact, there's a detailed history written on the back of the menu."

Standing there, Jonah thought of the life his grandmother once led. How he had been aware of his Jewishness only once. Sixth grade, when in a bathroom someone threw pennies at him. How little he'd understood even then.

"Oh, right," the waiter said, and fumbled through the pockets of his apron. "Before I forget, you dropped this when you went to the bathroom. It's your lucky day." He held up the button: blue and brown, chipped in a corner, two button-holes forming a face. "I should ask for double the tip. Nothing is free around here. But you know that as well as I do. Don't you, my brother? Finders keepers, losers weepers."

The waiter winked. Jonah blinked twice. He looked again at the waiter's paste-on Jew curls and black hat, the sly smile, the sallow skin. The magic, reappearing button twirled between his fingers like a shiny coin.

"How much do you want for it?" Jonah asked.

The waiter sighed. "Oh, but I can't put a price on such a treasure. I'll tell you what. Do for me a Jewish dance and it's yours."

"That button isn't yours to barter with," Jonah said.

The waiter pulled out a phone and swiped it on. Music started playing. It was the Havah Nagilah.

"What's yours is mine," he said, smiling, humming along with the music. He held the button up to his face and looked through one of its button-holes. He squeezed it into a fist. "We're brothers, remember? You and I, we're cut from the same cloth."

Jonah shoved the torn photo at the waiter and wrenched the button from his fist before stumbling away and out the door.

~

That night, button in tow, Jonah caught the next train to Krakow. He disputed the credit card charges from *RussianLove.com* and found a cheap hotel near the bus station. In the morning he went to Auschwitz, where he retraced his steps to the barracks called Kanada. It was dry and quiet and he was tired. The buttons he had seen the first time were buried and gone. He checked to make sure the coast was clear, then wedged the magic, reappearing button back into its place in the soil.

Almost as if on cue, Jonah heard a piercing whistle. He swung around and met eyes with a security guard on a Segway, rolling forward and then back. He had a long face and dark sideburns. He was wearing thick round sunglasses, which he pushed up the bridge of his nose. His uniform was numbered: one hundred seventy-five. His name, Zelinska, was sewn on the front. Jonah felt himself grow cold, even though the sun was fierce, tinting the soil yellow.

"No touching," the guard said.

"Sorry," Jonah said. "My mistake." He held his hands out to show they were empty. On the other side of the barbed wire fence, a man walked by, peering in.

"Where are you from?" the guard asked.

"America. New Jersey."

The guard hiked his pants and fidgeted with the radio that dangled from his belt. "A long way from home," he said.

"Yes," Jonah said.

"And are you looking for something?"

Jonah hesitated. He thought of every face he wouldn't recognize. Of every word he'd never say. He peered down at the ground beneath his feet and let out a big breath. Finally, he shook his head.

"Not even a button?"

"I don't understand," Jonah said.

"Your shirt," the guard said.

"My what?" Jonah looked down at his cream-linen short sleeve. One of the buttons was missing.

The guard rolled his Segway forward. He gestured to the spot in the soil where Jonah had wedged the magic button. "Is that it?"

Jonah said no, until he realized that it was. White. Four button holes. Pearly. He leaned down to pick it up.

"You're very lucky," the guard said.

Jonah admitted that he was, but by then the guard had spun his Segway around and rolled off.

JANA ROSE

OTHERWORLD

I met you when I was too young to know about what
a man could do to a woman, the difference between love
and sex. You took me into your studio and pretended you
needed a secretary, not a model. I worked for you in pencil
skirts, short heels, neat collared shirts I'd ironed the night
before. I wore scarves of turquoise and apricot.

That first day, when you held out your hand to mine,
asked me if I'd like a glass of water, did you know it all then?
Did you have it planned? Were you looking for a muse?

This is what I do now, after you: I take the travel paths
into the city. It took me a long time to get used to the sharp
metal hoods that protect us from the Burns. We're all like
rats now, crawling underground; the government never
allows us to let our faces see the sun. I sit in dark restaurants
with artificial light, ordering rum-and-cokes. When a man
offers to buy me a drink, I turn him down, thinking of you.
Thinking of what we used to drink in your studio, after one
of our sessions. A strange mix of Campari and vermouth
you devised, the "Otherworld Drink," you said.

I was too young then to know that you had basically
stolen me, made it so that no one else would ever match
you. You had stared at me for such a long time, sketched
every curve, made my lips plump and ripe as a melon in
your drawings. When I came over to see a draft, you seemed
shy—it was the only time I'd seen you doubtful about
yourself. And then you'd lead me to the bedroom, peel off
the same red robe all the other models had worn, lay me on
your bed, kiss me from ankle to neck. There was something
about my skin, you said. Something about my youth. By that

time, my every pore had blossomed like a flower, puckered in order to greet you, to take you inside me. I let out girlish, high-pitched moans. I wanted you every time. I could never have said no. I wanted you so far within me that you could live there, only your arms outside to hold me while I slept.

They called you a genius. But I had no idea who you were—just the artist who had hired me as an assistant three days a week, who one day complained he lost a model, could I help? I hadn't even seen your installations before then. I hadn't even tried.

After I left your studio those evenings, I went back to my mother. Did you ever think to ask? Did you ever want to know? She was fragile and greying in her bed, her only company a few books of poetry. When she got desperate she read nursery rhymes, and then even fairy tales. It was odd, seeing a grown woman with the Burns sitting up in bed reading a book with a cartoonish picture of Sleeping Beauty on the cover. It didn't make sense that soon she would leave me, that already she needed help to the bathroom, at times was so weak I had to feed her.

I never told you any of this: that on the nights I stayed late to have sex with you, she fell asleep in her bed with her bedside lamp on, hungry, without dinner. That there was no one to care for her while I was at your studio. That there were old pastels hanging in our house, paintings of houses and trees and shrubbery she had made when she was in college. She had wanted to be a painter. Instead, the man who seduced and got her pregnant left her alone, escaping somewhere—to California, she said. She hadn't known his last name or his address.

I was her reward.

~

Where did you get the idea for "Otherworld"? I never asked. Although later, it seemed so obvious, not magical or inventive at all. The sun had reached its peak; most people couldn't go out anymore without protective clothing. The beaches closed down, big black fences went up to keep people out, police and guards ushered people out of state parks. People built additions on their houses, tried to find ways to be outside without being in the sun. Kids stopped walking to school and stayed home to learn. Most of our world was online, in the Vision Fields.

And then there you came, the savior, the artist, using vast enclosed spaces to create a fake ocean, little drops of water landing on the palms of voyeurs' hands. The sound of crickets chirping at night, a cool breeze wafting through the factory room or a gallery that had commissioned you to show your work. It was like childhood, everyone said. It was like another world. But it was just our world from years ago, before the Burns. You'd found a way to make people happy again, to inspire them. Even, I think at times, to have hope.

I never wanted to leave you. I wanted to live in that world. I wanted to be in that place, in the whisper of your imagination, forever.

~

"Anya," my mother said, one Saturday night after I'd fed her applesauce and some other kind of mush the men had delivered earlier that day. "It's not going to be much longer."

She had spoken so little that week, had needed so much more rest. When I came home from your studio, she was in a restless sleep and didn't want to eat dinner. I always told her how busy we were, how much you needed me. I don't think she ever suspected that I spent the last two hours of my workday under your spotlight, then in your bed.

"How do you know?" I asked her. People took a long time to die from the Burns. For her, it had been six years. But I knew people could live up to ten, as long as they had help.

"I feel something coming through the air at me. Something breaking down a wall." She reached her hands up as she said this, into the empty space before me. She was hallucinating, I figured. And that seemed as sure a sign as any that things were coming to a close.

I didn't think I'd mourn too much when she was gone. She had been so much to work with, such a heavy weight. I had lived with the reality of her impending death for a long time.

That night, in her sleep, she passed. I slept in the chair and when I woke up, I felt the difference in the room. I looked to her stomach and saw she was no longer breathing. I sat there for a while, looking at her hands by her sides, which were solid and limp and fleshy. So still and pale. She had used them so recently to open the pages of a book, to reach out into the air. But now they lay there like pieces of furniture.

It wasn't until a few hours later that I called the undertaker to come and get her. I spent the rest of that day in the chair, inspecting every corner of the room, every crevice or design on the wallpaper she may have looked at on the days she waited for me to come home. I pulled the sheets off her bed and threw them into the trash. I tidied up, dusted, put loose books back in a neat stack on the shelf. I found glasses filled halfway with water, a bowl and spoon left from my feeding her soup or applesauce. Her presence somehow lingered, even though it was no longer in her body. I could feel the stuffiness of the room, her thick breath in the air, the kind of musk that develops when the windows have been so long closed.

On Monday, I dressed as usual to come to work. I didn't tell you anything was different, and you didn't seem to notice. After you sketched me, legs spread, tips of fingers reaching into my mouth, one hand on my inner thigh, you didn't take me to your bedroom. You approached me slowly, pulled me off of the stool so I fell on hands and knees. You kissed inside me, let your tongue move in curlicues around my ass, flick into my anus. After you fucked me that way, you turned me over and draped my legs over your shoulders. You told me I was the sweetest cunt you ever had. I told you I never wanted to go home.

For a whole week, I didn't.

~

What do you think about now, when you remember me? Or do you remember me at all? Have you had so many models in your studio, so many muses, that my image is only a few sketches in a stack of papers, some unknown girl in your paintings, hanging on the walls of a last museum?

I was young, is what I'm trying to tell you, though you knew. I hadn't known anything about sex before. I had been confined to my mother's house for almost all of my adolescence. Boys only existed in the Vision Fields. But when my mother's hospital bills got to be too much, and I needed to quit school and get a job, I found you so easily. I never thought you'd hire me. How many girls did you interview first? What was it you liked and wanted in me?

I'll never get to ask you these questions, but they are always in my mind, hovering between thoughts about what I'm going to eat, or when I'll finish a term paper, or whether I'll attend a gallery show. When a man tries to touch me, to smile and show an interest, I always appear rude, thoughtless, arrogant. What I can't explain to him is that I'm only for you. I don't know how to be anybody else's. I'm sure none of your girls do.

~

I was the one to be the first human in your installation. It was my idea, remember? A fairy, I suggested. Or a wood gnome. Anything you wanted. I'd dance and twirl mechanically, flitter out of people's grasps when they walked on the painted trails. Nude, I told you.

"I don't know if that would be possible," you said back to me, your tongue between my bare breasts. "They might call it pornography. Shut me down."

The government had grown wary of art, had made it difficult for you to even find a place to build your installations. They were causing mayhem, an official told you. They were making people see what they could no longer have.

But the next day, you said you wanted to try. You'd paint my body to blend into the bushes. I could be a ghost, barely visible, gone before someone fully turned his or her head. Viewers wouldn't know if they really saw me or not. And it would give an ethereal quality to the art, something that had been missing.

Your voice was booming, the joy on your face palpable. But you told me I couldn't stay over anymore. I had to go home. My presence was too much of a distraction. You had to work.

What you didn't know was that I hid in the hallway, wondering if I'd hear another woman's footsteps approach. Eventually, late into the evening, I did. She wore a long burgundy jacket, black high heels of a quality I could never afford. You opened the door to her. I heard muffled laughter, saw her lower the jacket so you could see her bare breasts. You leaned to her nipple and sucked like a lion. Hungry, like a baby.

My heart broke. First my mother's death, and now you.

If I had friends, they'd probably have said I should forget about you, find a new job, tell you I couldn't do Otherworld. But that's not what I decided. I was so lonely, so restless, so needy for you. I'd take you any way I could get you, even if I had to share. You knew this, I'm sure of it now. It's why you picked me. It's probably part of the magic you said I had: my inability to distance myself from you, my innocence, my loyalty. Whatever you want to call it. I was yours, but you weren't mine. Strangely, I kind of liked it that way. It made you more alluring.

~

I had my mother's body converted to ash. There was no space in the ground to bury people anymore, unless you had an excess of money. I stood in the crematorium and they let me watch as her body burned. I wanted to see. I wanted to remember something I had heard once, when I was a child, when I had been drawn for a time to religion. We come from ash, and to ash we return. It was like the schoolgirl's rhyme, *Ashes, ashes, we all fall down.* For some reason, those messages comforted me. All would eventually pass, so it didn't make sense to take myself so seriously, to think I was important. If my mother's body, my mother's presence and all the history it held, could become so grainy and small, my pain could, too.

I wanted to trust you. I wanted to call you "my darling." I wanted you to be only mine. But all you wanted was to compose and fuck me.

~

Even you were surprised by how much money we raised to build Otherworld. You had thought you were at the end of your career. You insisted the government was going to lock you up, close you down. The last museum had shut its doors in early November, though a few sculptures still haunted the central floor. Otherworld was set to surface there the following July in an old abandoned wing where paintings used to hang.

We practiced my part. You painted my body—dark blue with threads of gold. You took your paintbrush and tickled my shoulders and arms and back with liquid, and you put on music in the studio and asked me to dance. I hadn't danced since I was a girl, holding my mother's hand in our living room, listening to records—Otis Redding was her favorite. *That's how strong my love is, darling. That's how strong my love is.* That's when I missed her most, when my body hurt to have lost her. I put my sadness into my dance. I turned my hips and raised my arms and tried to lure you— an ancient goddess capturing the hero. For a few minutes, you danced along, taking my hands and twirling me. It was like we entered a vacuum in space, a different time, a vortex where it was only me and you, in the sun, in the gold, by the real water. If that was how people felt in your installation, I thought that maybe God had put me on the earth so I could dance for you, for the people, in my painted forest fairy costume. Back and forth, back and forth. Shuffle forward, shuffle back. Spin. Spin.

Then I opened my eyes, and we were back to the room again, and I felt sad. I showered the paint off in your bathroom, and I went home.

~

When the day for Otherworld's release arrived, the line reached out of the museum's wing all the way onto the next city block. Dozens of articles had appeared announcing the oncoming installation; all over the Vision Fields people were talking. I had purposely kept the Vision Fields silent in my house, refusing to log in but instead to read a book for a quiet hour at the end of my day. We were so busy getting Otherworld together, and I was tired. I read my mother's copy of *Little Red Riding Hood* thinking you were like the Big Bad Wolf, wanting me. I read *Cinderella*, wondering what parts of myself I would cut off for you, to have you inside me again. I was nervous about disappointing you, about not being the fairy you envisioned and wanted. When I told you this part, you said you didn't worry at all—I was perfect in every way. I held those words like an amulet, repeating them over and over in my mind. I suspected no one else in my life would ever say that to me. And I was right. Since you left, no one has.

I got to the installation early in the morning, even though it didn't open until just after lunch. You had high-level donors come first and walk through, to get a special tour. I stood in the preparation room and stripped off my clothes, all except my pale underwear, not caring about the mechanics who walked through, the chill moving from their quick breaths and movements. I was past fear of showing my body—I wanted to be seen. I raised my arms high and you dipped the paint in the can, covering one leg first, then the other, first in deep blues and purples that swirled together, then with strips of gold. You covered my underwear, the nipples of my breasts, then reached for a smaller paintbrush to cover my face. The only thing that would be left untouched was my hair, amber blonde, flowing out from my head, the one sign that I might be partly human.

I watched you as you worked and wanted to kiss you. I would have done anything. I would have given my body in any way you wanted it. But the installation was your baby. Your entire life seemed focused on having the exhibit go off as planned—not on me at all.

~

Someone on the set rang a bell, and we knew it was time to begin. There would be no music in the installation, just the sounds of nature—the rushing of ocean waves in the Sea Room, crickets and birds chirping in Forest Haven. I would have to listen and dance to the music in my head. I hid behind trees. Couples holding hands pointed out tiny details you had included to impress people, like the ivy growing on tree barks, or the crunch of pebbles on the ground through the walkway.

I began to let Otis Redding sing in my ear and I swayed my hips as I peeked behind one tree, then skipped to another, and another. It wasn't until I had done it a few times that I heard the gasps—was it fear or delight?—from the voyeurs. I laughed—I couldn't help it, and there was more reaction from the group. When I tired, I rested behind one of the trees in the back, letting the foam soil on the ground roll between my toes. I spent all day darting among trees, laughing melodically, dancing and turning, feeling cleansed, feeling whole under the stares of others. I felt I had never before been seen like that. It was the way I had been seen by you, only better, because there were more eyes, a bigger gaze, a greater perception of who I was.

I learned a lesson, being the muse in your installation: I only existed for others to see.

~

When the government shut you down two months later, they hardly gave any notice. It was an afternoon we were both in the office. A man came to the door with a letter; there were police behind him. If you didn't shut down Otherworld, which they had termed "obscene," you would be arrested. You stood at the door for a while, your eyes getting glassy, and I stood next to you, thanking them and guiding you away. We sat on the red couch you'd led me to that first day I met you. I wanted you to cry on my shoulder but you seemed in shock, frozen.

"What are you going to do?" I asked, knowing it was likely my body, my cackle, the dancing—just my presence in the exhibit—that was the root of your despair.

You just shook your head.

"I'm sorry," I said.

You looked at me then, a wisdom in your eyes, a kindness, even tenderness. But without lust. I missed the lust. I had hoped it would come back after that week we spent together, but it never had. I assume that once I became a piece of art, I was an object for you, something you made, something already figured out.

"They would have found a way to shut this down no matter what," you said. One of the longest sentences I'd heard from you in a while.

On the way home that night, I stopped at a bar, ordered a glass of wine, trying to feel grown-up. I would be losing my job—that much I knew. My future was up in the air. On the Vision Field behind the bartender, a man and a woman talked about your art, talked about the papers that had been delivered to your house that day. Nothing was too personal anymore, I noted. Nothing could be understood and dealt with in private, even when a person wanted it to be.

Except in the darkness of Otherworld's forest, I realized, where I had been painted, where I had been covered up. Where I was most buried, I also felt the most free.

~

You were not at the studio when I opened the door the next day. I entered your living area and saw that small things were missing—your coffee mug, a few stray clothes that you always had draped over a chair. In the bathroom, your toothbrush gone. The paints were absent, the charcoal, the drawing paper you'd always used to sketch models. On the small table where you usually left your breakfast dishes I saw a note, scribbled hastily.

Let them take it, it said. *I did everything I set out to do.*

I knew then that it was all over—the Otherworld exhibit, your career, my job. Any time you tried to do art in the future, you'd get papers, warnings, notes. Maybe you'd change your name, dye your hair, work in a different country from now on. I only wish that I'd known it all the last time I'd seen you, so I could have told you how I felt.

Maybe you would have taken me with you. I could have brought you to my house, even though the loan collectors were calling. I loved that you had defied the government—I wanted to help you. But perhaps the way the artist worked now was as shapeshifter, as renegade. In the new world, a true artist could not have a peaceful life.

What saved me from anyone knocking on my door was that no one had seen my face. No one would ever recognize my body, covered daily in clothes. I was a walking daydream.

I wanted a note from you, something addressed to me, but when the reporters came to the studio, I simply showed them what you wrote. I knew that was what you wanted.

I went home that night and looked at you on the Vision Fields, reading everything I could find. I went to sleep with my fingers between my legs.

~

It wasn't long after you left that I enrolled in college, the only option I had. The loans I took out would keep the creditors away and help me to keep my mother's house. I worked in a small café, making coffee drinks for professors and students, the kind of people who remembered your work. I decided I would study, I would read, I would wait to hear from you. Someday, maybe I'd find you myself. I didn't know how to get a message to you, but I thought of you every night before bed and every morning when I woke up, my dreams hazy, always, with your image.

And one day, with whatever I'd inherited of my mother's talent, with my memory of my fairy, dancing self, I would become an artist, just like you.

Jamie Etheridge

When We Saw Sparks

He used to say that Adel was so close to hell you could see sparks. So that's where we buried him, in Sparks, in the cemetery behind the church with the rich, red Georgia clay piled on top of his silver bullet coffin and his face like wax.

I was fourteen and didn't realize when I kissed his cheek at the wake that it wouldn't be soft, warm, flesh but something cold and hard, arctic where once summer bloomed. I can feel it still, that frozen flesh, the death of my childhood.

It rained too, as all good summer days in the South, and we had to hurry, the pallbearers working up a sweat as they rolled his coffin out of the hearse and onto their shoulders and then up, over the clumps of grass and wildflowers growing at the edge of the cemetery.

There must have been a graveside service, a preacher we didn't know speaking about a man he never knew. But I don't remember it.

Instead, all I see is the grass carpet they've used to cover the mound of earth. It slants to one side, the dirt poking through and blades of grass drip morning dew into the hole where they'll bury my father.

To distract myself, I think of nursery rhymes: *Little boy blue the sheep's in the meadow come blow your horn when the bough breaks all the king's men and Jill came tumbling down.*

The smell of honey overpowers me but then I realize it isn't honey. It's gardenias and more specifically the faux gardenias of my grandmother's favorite Avon perfume, a perennial best seller she wears even to funerals, apparently.

I gag, too loudly, and my mom gives me a quick, harsh

look. So I suck in air and swallow the vomit on my tongue. More than thirty years later, I still get nauseous every time I smell jasmine or gardenias.

A faint sprinkle starts toward the end of the service and the smell of rain and fresh cut grass washes away the heavy perfume enough so that I can breathe. I stand up, gather my younger siblings and follow behind my mother as she heads to where the cars are parked.

He was forty-five, with seven children, the youngest just turned two.

I want to shout out—the numbers seem important. But everyone's hot and sweaty, ready for the mounds of food waiting back at granny's house.

As we reach the parking lot, I pause and look back to see two workers standing next to the casket. One, in faded jeans and grease stained shirt, is working a crank, a giant rusted wheel that's attached to the levers that will lower the coffin into the grave.

The other, a man about my father's age, though thinner and wearing a baseball cap, is smoking a cigarette and laughing, as if he just told the funniest joke in the world. When he looks up and sees me staring, his smile drops and he looks down at his hands, the cigarette trailing smoke.

JENNI GARBER

TWICE A WEEK

My therapist, who's eighty-seven, is working so far past the age of retirement that my fear over walking into his office and finding him dead in his armchair sent me straight to a second therapist to deal with how worked up I was over the first therapist, who, surely, any day now, I will absolutely find dead in the armchair in his office.

My therapist doesn't exist without compression socks. Without slippers, without a wrist wrapped in one of those metal, medical bracelets. Without khaki shorts pulled to the very zenith of his belly, his belt stretching like the equator line around a globe.

And every other month, a plump and purple eye from a stumble down the stairs.

I've realized, there is a benefit in seeing a therapist who requires an inhaler after the twelve-step walk from office to bathroom, a trip he takes at least three times each fifty-minute session, requiring him to break into my self-obsessed monologue with a "Hold that thought. Got to make a pit stop."

A therapist who is eager for book and movie recommendations (anything with Jennifer Lawrence). Who is present enough to jot those down, yet never makes notes on sessions, including medications, thus reliably forgets which prescriptions he's prescribed and how often.

Who, in general, manages to forget a third of what's said, meaning I get to use the same anecdotes over and over, to amuse him, but more importantly, myself.

I need a therapist who'll stomach my confessions, the thoughts and the acts, then still welcome me back for the following week. A therapist who can relate to how I worry that my thoughts and my acts will mean he won't welcome me back for the following week.

A therapist who can relate in general. Who spent time in Panama as a military psychologist, so after hearing a story about my mom abandoning my sister in Panama for six days, rocks in his seat a few times, builds inertia till he tips to a standing position, stumbles to the cabinet, uses one hand to brace himself and the other to pull out books until he finds one of his maps, and soon our chairs are together and we're watching a YouTube documentary on his laptop about the history of the Panama Canal.

What could be better for my confidence than a therapist who is eager to see me each session, because I'm the only person he knows who can help him download a smartphone app? Who allows me to think he moves the potted flowers around the office just to see if I'm paying attention.

Who, on day one, was up-front about not accepting my insurance (what they pay isn't worth the paperwork, he says), but instead of sending me out the door lets me write checks for what I can, when I can. This courtesy was extended, even after I made the mistake of asking if he saw mostly kids, basing the assumption on the cartoonish self-portraits all over the walls. But, obviously, as he was quick to correct, these were not paintings by kids but by adults, just adults without any artistic training. And he didn't hold that against me. At least, that's what I told myself when he led me into the office for the first time, waving me away from the inviting couch and instead into a straight back, armrestless, cushion-needing chair.

And any time I ask about a book, one of the dozens with titles like, *Psychotherapy and Judaism*, lining the wall behind his very comfy-looking chair, behind the little table with the tissue box and tobacco pipe he never smokes, in his office on the second story of his nice Chicago house, he says, "Don't know haven't read it," and I respect how he never lies or makes something up. How he doesn't even seem to have that urge.

My problem with arriving too early is made even more awkward because I have the first appointment of the day, and even more so, because he works where he lives, so I always try to be obnoxious with the front door, loud as possible going up the carpeted stairs and down the hallway past his office door, then past the closed bathroom door, to the two-chair waiting room, but I still end up shocking his wife when she wanders out of the bathroom, humming, a bent-over woman in a robe, curlers, with a mug of steaming oatmeal, the handle of the spoon sticking out.

It doesn't help that when I get to the waiting room I already feel guilty for being forty minutes early, and for some reason it seems better not to turn on the waiting room light and draw attention to myself, but to just sit as quietly as possible, in the dark, and wait to be noticed.

When this happens I make it up to my therapist by giving him a dream to analyze. He wakes up for dreams.

Our relationship is very give and take.

My therapist reins in my rants when necessary, spools in my mania with a sobering, "Dude . . ." Or an even sterner, "You're talking about animals again."

My therapist reaffirms my experiences, my outlook on the world with an at-the-ready "This is why I can't eat before our sessions."

Who, when I say, "I don't think I can talk about it in front of you," replies gruffly, "What? You want me to leave the room?"

Who keeps me from deflecting, from asking about his day by saying, "That's not why you're here."

Or sometimes, goes so far as to whip out the, "Dude, you're really fucked up. You should probably see someone about that."

Inkwell Interview
Melissa Febos: Writing Without a Net

Melissa Febos's memoir and essays face their gale-force emotional winds as if it were her job to describe them without blinking. Her breakout memoir *Whip Smart*, published in 2010, offered readers a sensational subject— she had worked as a dominatrix in a sex "dungeon"— but stunned them with clear, lucid self-examination that transformed that material into art. Her 2019 essay collection, *Abandon Me*, examines an tormented romantic relationship that she began writing about even as the experience was still unfolding. Memoirists, beware: that's called flying without a net, as there is no guarantee the author will ever reach the insight needed to complete the book's arc. The gift of insight coupled with poetic prose established Febos as one of the best memoirists now writing. She is a rare writer who can put her mind on dual tracks, observing her experience even as she is living it, revising and crafting until the experience transcends itself on the page. What does that even mean? Read her work, read our conversation, and find out.

Lori Soderlind: Your work generates a lot of adjectives such as "fierce".

Melissa Febos: Raw.

Soderlind: Raw, that's a good one. Excellent . . . *Whip Smart* is the story of working as a dominatrix in a dungeon in Manhattan for four years, and it leads to exploring a lot of questions about addiction, sex, power—a lot of compelling and often really dark subjects, but I'm also interested in the beauty that seems to arise from those experiences. My students and I have been noticing that lately the culture seems to be allowing us to discuss things that might have not long ago been considered sentimental. In your work, particularly as I moved out of *Whip Smart* and started reading *Abandon Me*, I noticed your willingness to talk about love, what love actually means. You know, not just need, but love. What I'm wondering, if we're reading you correctly, is whether those things are really what you're getting at when you're talking about the raw, fierce things.

Febos: You mean, need and love.

Soderlind: Need and love. Things that I think ten years ago we weren't allowed to talk about. They were too squishy.

Febos: I mean, I can't speak for the culture at large. But for me, certainly ten years ago, I didn't have access to the kinds of love that I do now. I think for a lot of us, there's this organic movement through need to love, right? Which I guess mimics infancy. Only when we become autonomous, integrated individuals are we capable of experiencing love that's not predicated on dependency. I think if they're looked at as a continuum of my development as a person, which I think that they can be, my books . . . *Whip Smart* is very much about the dynamics I had to move through in order to get to a more direct examination of love, attachment, vulnerability, and what those things would have meant to risk something in relationships, right? So it's power games, and performance, and ways of enacting desire and connection in the self that are fractured. Where you can just inhabit a part of yourself, and maybe perform it for an audience where the stakes are lower... What a lot of us do—even if you're not in a dungeon, or on heroin—I think what we do in our young relationships, we're performing aspects of ourselves that we feel comfortable being, or that we wish that we were, that we can't escape.

And then *Abandon Me* is about moving through to an idea of love, like really getting down to the bone of dependency and the way that I looked at it as synonymous with love, and I think the way that our culture at large looks at it. Or at least, what capitalism has done to sell it to us as need and dependency, and how this idea of love that we have, that we were sort of raised on at least in terms of media and marketing, is very much about a really sort of unhealthy, ungenerous, wounded, insatiable need, and not about generosity and agency and care.

Soderlind: In *Whip Smart*, you're going through this journey about awakening to power, growing up in certain ways, and coming to adulthood and power. It seems like *Abandon Me* is kind of continuing that journey into being able to see these experiences as things you pass through to learn what actual love is. Do you think you arrive there in *Abandon Me*? Do we ever answer that question?

Febos: No, I don't think I arrive there, at least not in what I covered in the book. I think I moved through what I needed to. *Abandon Me* ends on the precipice of it. In *Abandon Me* I went all the way to the end of the kind of love that love songs are about, poems are about, and tragedies are based on. It was all of that need, dependency, and the stakes felt incredibly high all the time, it was a very selfish and desperate situation. It was very romantic in the sense that it was like living within a story that wasn't built on a foundation of actually knowing or caring or considering the other person or even seeing them. You're just sort of projecting your stories onto each other. I think it was the complete failure of that kind of love. It was all of the secret desires of my heart, which were to be showered in gifts, to fly all over the country, to get crazy love letters, to have poems written about me, and it was living hell. Literally hell.

I've documented a lot of this in *Whip Smart*, but I've been through other kinds of hell and this was worse. That apex of romantic love. It was the most miserable two years of my life. That story ends on the moment when I step in the other direction. Not this next book, but the next one will be what happens after that.

Soderlind: This is one of the really interesting things about being a serial memoirist. There are different ways to do it, but in some cases we watch a person developing this unfolding awareness on the page. It's not like you shouldn't write this until you're finished, because when you're finished you're dead. We are going to keep unfolding.

Febos: That's what I tell my students all the time. The only real story's end is when you die. That's it. There's only one ending to the story. And that's it, as far as I know.

Soderlind: Well, I suppose if maybe the Buddha arrived. But if we are always in the process of deepening, it means that every book that comes before is its own perfect statement of what was. I'm presuming that readers are also on journeys.

Febos: My partner has a poem. She actually has a series of poems that are all titled, "Every moment I've been alive I've been at the height of my powers" and it sounds like, "Oh yeah!" But, it's actually a literal statement, every moment

I've been alive I've been at the height of my powers. I'm the most perfect version of myself at every moment that I'm living, I'm doing the best that I can. I think that's true about my work as well. *Whip Smart* is almost unbearable for me to look at sometimes because I've changed so much. I started writing it when I was 26. My memories, my experiences of it, my styles of sentences have evolved since then. Yet, it's my first baby. It was the best thing I could possibly write at the time. It was far beyond my capabilities. I think that's true of both my books. They were by far the best things I've ever written and actually transcended my talent at the time because it was a story I needed to tell. So, my skill level had to rise to meet the material I needed to create.

Soderlind: It's fascinating sometimes to watch writers become interested in a topic that, consciously or not, is going to be "their topic." I know personally, my first book was a road trip book and my second book is a road trip book. I didn't mean to do that. And what's really funny to me about that, when I realized what I'd done, I'd re-written the first book fifteen years later with changed insights. I realized I couldn't write the same book again if I tried, and yet, it was the same outline of a book with a new story and new insight.

Febos: I think that's one of the most beautiful revelations of the memoirist, not only can we usually not avoid writing about the same things but we ought not even try. That's part of our job. It is to enact this evolution of self and ideas and of style on the page by churning things over. I look at my favorite writers who are writing in multiple styles over and over. I'm thinking of Jeanette Winterson who is one of my favorite writers. If you look at her early work, it's of crazy, fabulous stories like, *The Passion* and *Written on the Body,* and I remember when she published her memoir finally, so much of her previous books were in that. She was digesting, fighting, and healing from her own life and her past. I think every artist is doing that in their own way. For me, I want to know that my relationship to the largest events in my life and my obsessions are going to change, evolve, and grow. That's so comforting to me.

Soderlind: I tell my students all the time that one of the most challenging parts of being a successful memoirist is transforming your material. I mean you could write the facts down, but actually transforming that into art and succeeding at that, it's really hard. It's asking you basically to have some deep personal insight. It's like you sit down in the beginning and you start writing and you realize by the time the thing is finished, unless it's gonna get thrown out, you better have arrived at something about yourself.

Febos: I think that's the thing people don't quite know they are signing up for, and maybe that's a good thing. I think people writing in other forms have to do this too, some more than others. You know most of my friends are writers, my partner's a writer. I've definitely seen her with a book of poetry, very clearly with a set of challenges, and come out at a different location in her relationship to them. With a memoirist it's so specific, you pick at the beginning the things you are going to grow around and then write your way into a change. You hear people say that you should be really far away from the things you write as a memoirist. That's not true for me at all, partly because I have a horrible memory. So I'm always in a race against my own memory. If I was trying to write *Whip Smart* today, it would be so impressionistic because I wouldn't remember anything. For me the drive to write is a drive to understand an aspect of my own experience, and it's usually pretty soon after something has happened.

I started writing *Abandon Me* while I was still in the primary relationship that I write about over the course of that book. I was in it. I think I started writing about it as a way to survive it psychically: "I have to transform this into something meaningful." I couldn't bear the idea of being in that much pain for no reason. "Well, if I'm going to be living in this emotional hell I'm at least going to make an aesthetic object out of it." I had a really interesting moment when I was two-thirds of the way through the title essay of the book, which really confronts the relationship that the book is structured around. There was a moment, I was in an artists' residency . . . and I was still in the relationship. She and I were actually fighting on the phone nightly and I'm in this artists' colony in the woods and I was waving my phone around trying to get a signal so we could continue fighting. And I'm trying to save the relationship. It was like that thing, you know, when your psychic claws are all the way in. There was no way for me to put it down. Then I would be in my studio in the morning, and I remember I had all my little note cards up, I was telling the story, and at that point I was planning that at the end of the book it would be a happy ending. We were going to end up together, because that's what I was going to make happen in my life.

I remember having this moment; I was fully in my writer brain so I was thinking on behalf of the story . . . I was totally in the beautiful self-forgetting of creating something and looking at it structurally. I thought the correct ending to this story is that she, the narrator me, leaves her. Obviously, there's no other correct ending to this story. Then I was like, "Whoa." So in that way it was weird, it was like art telling me and being a more truthful mirror than my own mind for what was going on in my life.

Soderlind: Something a little mystical about the creative process when that happens. As it happens, my recent book too, didn't have an ending, until I ended a relationship. Stumbling upon that, I was like, "That was *not* the book I thought I was writing," but it's not fiction. That's the material. You don't have a choice, you can't say, "Wait a second, we can do redemption with a happy ending." But isn't redemption a lot more interesting with an unhappy ending?

Febos: In the end, the fact of it for me is, I am a really poor judge of what a happy ending is. I would've just fought to the death for what I thought was a happy ending, and in hindsight could not have been more wrong. The idea that I would still be with this person is a blackout, just thinking about it.

Soderlind: Has she read your book?

Febos: Yeah. Yes, she's read the book.

Soderlind: See, that question takes us out of the fascination with what it is to really write memoir and surprise ourselves on the page. That brings us into some reality questions about writing memoirs. Looking at your narrative character on the page, secrecy is this big theme that runs through a lot of your work. In fact the subtitle of *Whip Smart* is "A True Story of a Secret Life." There's a lot of secrecy in "Labyrinths," the essay we were talking about in class last night, talking about the secret self and hiding things. Then you write memoirs about all the hiding. How does it feel to share that?

Febos: I think one of the epigraphs of *Abandon Me* is a quote that I love, that I actually carried around with me. It was almost the epigraph of *Whip Smart* but it wasn't quite right. The quote is, "It is joy to be hidden and disaster not to be found." It was like the epigraph of my life. And probably would be an apt epigraph to anything I ever write. People are always saying, "Oh, you're so brave and you don't mind sharing yourself," or they think (memoirists) are the type of people who would spill our whole life story to someone on a bar stool or something. Actually, I've found that memoirists are often not like that. They are very private, very secretive people who feel hidden within themselves and maybe trapped with that. I think the thing to remember is that a memoir is not written with an audience, even if it's written with an audience in mind. A memoir is written in total solitude. So for me, my work could be described as a conversation I have alone with myself. It's the conversation I'm afraid to have with anyone else and so I can only have it alone with myself on the page. At the end of it, it's such a cathartic and meaningful experience that I want to share it, because I think when we walk through any kind of fire we want to show people how it was done. The curse of secrecy is thinking you're alone and you're the only one who has ever lived with that particular burden.

Soderlind: I think it takes a lot of confidence in what you have shared on the page with yourself, that you got it right. I have this terrible fear that my insights, once I've shared them with other people, will show me all the ways my insights were flawed, and I'll be like, "Oh, I didn't realize."

Febos: Well, I mean they will or they will try to. Every nasty thing I've ever thought about myself or my work I've read on the Internet. Critics have been very kind to me, but it's the Internet . . . Anyone publishing books today learns not to read Amazon reviews. I hold onto (my work) for a really long time, that's the beauty of writing, it's like one of the hardest things to do but no one has to see you fail. You get to (redo) it. We can practice it in privacy for as long as we need to before anyone ever sees us. Then we just emerge and look like an expert. But it's really hard. Every sentence in both of those books, particularly *Abandon Me*, I probably re-wrote 20 times.

Soderlind: So, switching gears, I talked to my students about the subjects of memoirs and what a memoir can do. I'm often telling them that you really don't have to have any kind of spectacular life experience in order to write a worthwhile memoir. On the other hand, your life experiences have been pretty intense. Melissa, you spent four years working in the dungeon and had addiction issues and were in all of these big, high concept kinds of things, but I bet you are going to agree with me, it doesn't have to be that way.

Febos: Totally.

Soderlind: But, how can we convince them after making a name and a career on huge experiences? I can see inside their minds, and I know that they are thinking: "What I'll do is spend a year living in a rat-infested tunnel."

Febos: I've been asked a lot of times if I've done things for the material and the answer is really honestly no, I have not. I really just made those choices because it seemed like a good idea at the time.

Soderlind: I think it's possible people do make life choices for the material, but I do not think that of you after reading your books.

Febos: I don't think it yields the kind of writing that I'm interested in reading, because I actually want to see the transformation on the page, and you can't schedule that. I do think the dominatrix stuff, maybe having a sea captain father, are not totally regular. But the addiction is one of the most normal things in the world, right? I'm sure everyone in this room has been touched by it.

Likewise mental illness. I think a huge part of being a memoirist or being a writer in general is, it's not about transmitting information about the exotic to people. I actually don't think people are very compelled by the exotic. I think that the most satisfying moment for a reader, I should speak for myself, the most satisfying moment for me as a reader is recognition. Right? When I read an articulation of something that I already know really deeply, that's deeply familiar to me, but that I've been unable to put words to, afraid to put words to or haven't even thought to name.

I recently read a friend's book and he articulated childhood as a hysterical, hyper-smart, really moody little artist child's experience and I was like, "Wow," because I just recognized it completely. So I actually don't think the things people connect to in *Whip Smart* have anything to do with the dominatrix stuff. Most of the people who I hear from about my work are people who don't share my concrete experiences but share the feelings of the mechanisms or the habitual stuff.

Soderlind: Although I think we have to acknowledge—and it's not interesting enough to do more than acknowledge this, I think—but there's the publishing pressure.

Febos: Yes, but you know what, it's a gross game . . . Nobody wanted to publish *Whip Smart.*

Soderlind: Really?

Febos: Really. Oh my God, it was rejected by over 40 publishers. There was only one offer and it was the last one. It's interesting because the book got a lot of attention, but people were like, "hmmm." First of all publishing is still run by a lot of old guard conservative folks, and though this is changing . . . they were like, oh yuck, that's yucky. I also think it wasn't the sensational tabloid story, it was a really unsexy book about sex. It was intellectual and feminist.

Soderlind: What do you think they were really allergic to in it? I think it was the feminism.

Febos: I think they were mis-marketing it in some ways. How do you promote an unsexy, feminist book about sex work?

Soderlind: Well, just like that.

Kevin LeMaster
Tether

i've never understood the rules;
    the smooth pole,

rope, rough as an unattached limb,
    drawn taut like a ship held by mooring.

the ball was a thicker leather,
    hard as the bodies we used to surrender

when we held each other in the dark,
    wrapped around and tethered. we are

much softer and gentler than the game we played
    as kids, striking the dark part of your thigh

with my firm hand, your warmth held tightly
    against its stroke.

Kevin LeMaster

Object Permanence

when i think of the C word
    i think of the mug
you brought me

a consolation prize for
    beating a disease
we cannot clearly name

those nights spent being burned alive
    by radiation, fanning through
your veins like wildfire

a neglected match struck against
    a killer's torch sends sickness
seeking solace in the dark cavern of

your body and finding none
    but this mug with all its
definitions of things that cancer cannot kill

still couldn't save you from your
    morning cup of coffee
another day spent

warming your uncovered head
    against a swollen sun
your gray skin fresh from treatment

pinking up like
    a young girl's blushing cheeks
you close your eyes like you did the

first time we kissed, because that's
    what you read good girls do
now wondering what you did

to deserve your body's abandonment
    like all the first times were
never enough for absolution

Laura Sobbott Ross

MERCURIAL

A catchall of current, the grocery store.
At a circulating point
on the conveyor belt, I find

an equilibrium. What tumbles out
is tagged and tracked. Couponed.
Yes ma'amed. Blipped on a barcode.
My parcel laid bare. An empty

plastic bag skitters blue across
a perfect welt of sunlight on terrazzo.
Plastic divider sticks pass
like batons between strangers.

There's so much breathing here:
the pears in their crisp skins,
the pistachios and the sangria,
the pork rinds and the brisket,
Alma, at the cash register,
Kurt, sliding a box of frozen peas
into a sack. There are eyes

in the potatoes. Egg yolks,
just a wobble in the dense stasis
of albumen: a dozen fragile ellipses;
wrap them carefully, please.

Once, I panicked in a Kroger.
A sudden sensory enjambment—
the shelves of Rice-a-Roni,
pickles, and creamed corn.

Leaving my cart in the aisle,
I swore I'd never come back.
Now, I wonder at all of us.
The slow drift. The beautiful ruin.
Our bruises and expiration dates.
The palpable softness of ripening.

Through the storefront window,
leaves rattle suddenly
from a high branch.
A brittle, radiant migration
no one seems to notice.

LAURA SOBBOTT ROSS
JIGSAW PUZZLE

FOR GEORGINA

You know the way it goes, a thousand
pieces, maybe more; you start with the sorting—
with what you can find in common.
        There are new faces
at the family vacation rental this summer:
children, spouses, lovers.

We share long, glowy hours, an ocean view,
a bond with the ones we already love.

A frame forms, first in delicate links.
Our fingers parsing through bread and linens,
oil for the skillet. Excuse me while I reach for

    that likeminded fragment, and let you
        finish the gist of my intention.
Isn't this the piece of tomato, the hat, the pagoda,
the redwood, the hummingbird throat you're looking for?
Nothing is seamless, but
    from across the lamplit table,
        we delight in our connections—
loops and sockets, tabs and blanks, a simple simpatico.

    But who cares what it's called?
It's the giddy progress that keeps us going at it;
it's what emerges beneath our casual efforts.

We'll refer back to the images on the box.
Billiard balls. Tiger lilies. Baby owls.
    A thousand small convergences
in our Niagara Falls, our fissured Eiffel Tower.

Alice B. Fogel

But If

but if it dawns on us
we might never get it right
angled we'll still spin through all
thirty two petals of the compass
rose   blown like slow tones into air
without vanishing   we hope
to slip between silence and its spellbound
black into invented reds   alleged yellows
and thank God it is always night
somewhere   a long chain
of dwindling notes or maybe
the gauntlet of implausibles   leads us to summer
in a high meadow where forty thousand moths
engorged with nectar are enough
to fill the grizzlies' hunger
for a day   if it isn't science it's instant myth
because otherwise   who would believe
one mouth could sing
in so many voices   so much sugar
carry on the breeze as if
we were each one in billions
of skewed moons whose choral light comes
from a singular point above

Alice B. Fogel

Glacial Consciousness

what bad shape reality must be in   when we can't predict
                        what genre we're looking at
        what scale or dimension   whether
to crawl or to fly   a chance of road   heavy veins
        flooded dendrite   or delta   go figure
                        because partly   we want to live
in this cognitive dissonance unseasonably taken to the vanishing
                        point but not so much in the spatial
        instability where we're forced to worship except on Sundays
weather's obsolete doctrine   what disturbs us is knowing
we go too far when we travel to somewhere we've never existed
                where we have to calibrate equally the record
        parameters of particle and star
country of mountains   country of deeps   the blood mystic
        reported in 3D   we pore over and over it
        dread   its beauty   go from slough
        of despond to the predictable   highs   stumbling
in and out of focus   in and out of our right mind
                        make our plans to wait out
        form   trending toward flow   a biomorphic
bellwether   clamoring   the velocity of glaciers
        dropping and not   always   clearing by dawn

J.A. Bernstein

Squad

It's possible that there isn't a more terrifying experience in the life of a North American, adolescent male than the tryouts for a middle school basketball team. Certainly, encounters with women, young and old, can alter a boy's standing, as can experimenting with alcohol, nicotine, pot, or other forbidden substances. In Zach Epstein's case, feeling up the leader of the drama club, and then, if the rumors are to be believed, reaching third base with her best friend, seven nights later, can account for his rise in popularity, though the real factor, as anyone versed in his situation could attest, was his ability to drive on Thomas Lang, he of the six-foot-two-inch frame and formidable wingspan, like some swatting Goliath, in scrimmage games up in the gym. It goes without saying that Zach would have been a first-round pick—the equivalent of a third or fourth draft choice—in any reasonable selection for the varsity Middle School squad.

This was, it should be said, for a team at what I'll call Chicago Academy, a private, K-12 school on Chicago's North Side, which I was then fortunate to attend, albeit with a family income trailing the vast majority of my peers. It also goes without saying that hookups and sex, while fervently wished for, and, one could suppose, on that rarest of occasion, attained, counted far less in the annals of achievement than earning a spot on that team.

The pecking order in our system was routinely and clearly defined by the tables at which one sat during lunch in the cafeteria. Among each gender, a "leaders' table" was ordained, where the seven most popular—eight, if one could fit—sat dutifully and quietly, appearing, to all the rest of us, to have a very good time. What they discussed at their tables was unclear: perhaps a history of their exploits, or backdoor cuts through the lane. It also goes without saying that these fourteen individuals, male and female alike, were either superstar athletes (in our terms), or physically beautiful, or both. There were exceptions. Some were quite pimpled and large and had managed to work their way in through sheer and brute force, usually in the form of taunting others, bullying, or otherwise hanging on. Their reign in these circles rarely lasted, and they usually filtered out to other tables, where they were joined by fellow aspirants, that is to say, the rest of us.

On a Monday afternoon in November, tryouts were held for the varsity squad in the upper-school gym, an enormous, cold, brick-walled arena reeking of Lysol and socks. We, the twenty-seven prospectives, began by forming two shaky lines on one end of the court, where we proceeded, in view of the glaring coaches, to perform basic layups and rebound. The goal was simply to see who could get the ball in, a reasonable proposition, since anyone who couldn't make a layup was without question condemned. The final roster for this team would, we well knew, include twelve individuals, of whom seven were fixed. That is, they dominated the competition, could score on their own, or otherwise possessed the height to rebound, which in middle school counted for a lot. They'd dubbed themselves the "Dream Team" collectively after the NBA stars who had rattled the Olympics that summer.

Zach Epstein, stud that he was, obviously began the procession. How he'd come to possess the ball first wasn't clear, nor for that matter contested. After all, he'd just returned from Barcelona, where he'd watched the Dream Team play. Zach, smiling glowingly, extending his tongue—

less a reference to Michael Jordan and his towering, jaw-drooping dunks than Zach's own propensity to extend that hot limb into rumored and imperceptible orifices—cradled the Spalding TF-1000, molested its seams, did a running two-step on a defender who wasn't there, dribbled between his knees, pirouetted, and barreled to the lane, where he proceeded to scoop the ball up, gently roll it out with his fingers while torquing his body and flexing his admirable frame—he was all of five-two but vigorously cut and inordinately, Spanishly tanned—and kiss it up towards the backboard, where it seemed to hold for a second, suspended in view of twenty-six beaming admirers—with the exception of Thomas Lang, who thought he was crap—and circled the rim and fell out.

Zach had missed. This didn't seem possible.

Zach of course took it in stride, jogging back sluggishly, limpingly even, as if he'd just injured himself attempting a dunk rating twelve on the difficulty scale. "Shiznit," he grumbled.

Zach wore the same requisite navy blue shorts and orange t-shirt as the rest of us, both stenciled Academy, though his had been expertly bleached, even ripped in places, so that they resembled the kind, say, Brandon Walsh wore on *90210*, then the girls' favorite show, which Zach himself claimed not to watch. He tugged his shorts, smiling obliquely, and shuffled to the back of the line. "Who's got dis?"

~

The odd thing about Zach Epstein is that he was so popular—mysterious, even—that he could afford to be friends with a person like me, someone who was so far below him psychosocially that it must have seemed glamorous to him to have me over at his house. (Picture Joseph Stalin greeting famished peasants, circa '28, and you have some idea of what I mean.) One Saturday morning, a couple months before the team tryout, he invited me over, ostensibly to help him with homework. We took Biology together, and though we didn't sit together in class—even magnanimity had its limits—we'd been friendly since youth, having endured Hebrew School together at a Conservative temple nearby. We'd drifted in and out of circles since then, and I'd moved to his school in sixth grade, after which we occasionally talked. Of course, he seemed to have his way with every girl in our class, and with whom I had barely shared words.

Still, earlier that summer, while Zach was seated courtside in Spain—and, it was rumored, eating tapas with Karl Malone—I had sat alone in the apartment of Jill Brandt, three inches across the couch from her, uncertain of how I should move. Her best friend, Erin Zoellick, had called me up and, after several puzzling and awkward exchanges, invited me to come over. Both girls were at about my rank—that is, not entirely foreign to the Leaders, though hardly within their spheres. Think of us as Estonia, or one of the non-medalling, early-round teams.

Here we sat, hands tightly folded in our own discreet laps, she in the threaded, gray turtleneck from J.Crew that every girl our age seemed to own, her walnut hair Scrunchied and barely diverting her bangs, which hung down resplendently to cover her delicate face. She had braces, of course, which she did her best to conceal; currently, she seemed to be frowning, her eyes fixed ahead on the living room's hulk of a set. I, meanwhile, in a flurry of emotion I hadn't previously encountered or felt, heard my heart racing like an actual Spalding pounding against the gym floor. We had been like this for twenty minutes, possibly more. And neither of us had moved. It was beyond the point of being awkward. I tried very hard not to fart, though I could feel my stomach gelling and winding into knots. I couldn't breathe.

Certainly I wanted to kiss her, less by force of sheer attraction than the desire to say I had, which, in some sense, is more powerful. She looked at me warily, as in, *who is this guy, why's he here?* Having come to the school in sixth grade, I might as well have been from outer space. Yet I could see her cheeks brighten, perhaps brushed with rouge, and the traces of liner she wore. It had obviously been important for me to come over, even if I hadn't—and wouldn't, it seemed—crossed that unfathomable divide.

Until this happened: out of the depths of the kitchen, Erin Zoellick emerged, laughing and raising her arms. "Come on, you two. Do I have to do *everything* for you?" Evidently, she'd been watching us for some time.

This from a girl who was at best four feet tall, and, though not physically developed by comparison, had the confidence and mien of some aged, Hollywood madam. She smiled at us sharply, with her short, angled, penguin-like face, her black hair cut in a bob, as was then in vogue, and her pale, furry arms reaching out. She proceeded to turn my whole head—by force, it seemed—towards Jill Brandt's. She did the same with Jill's, so that we were now facing one another rather than the hulking black set. She pushed our heads together, slowly at first, then with more force. Soon our two noses almost joined, our lips an inch apart, and we both heard her say, "Now you kiss." We did that, I suppose, though by this point I couldn't feel a thing, and the only recollection I have of that moment—what would, in fact, be my first kiss, and, in some sense, my last—is the smell of Jill's brown sofa, an enormous, ratty thing, and how it smelled kind of fetid, like shit, which might have been the churn in my gut but, in greater likelihood, stemmed from her cat, a ragged gray creature which leaped up onto the set, seemed to admire us from afar, cackle at us even, and then chase Erin off into the gloom of the hall.

Our kiss, or whatever you might call it, lasted half-a-second.

Twenty minutes later, I was home.

~

"So I heard you made out with Jill Brandt," Zach Epstein said to me, miraculously enough, several weeks later. We were studying in his basement, grouped around a white drafting table. His house was feverishly modern, with high, vaulted ceilings, plush carpets, and firehouse stairs. It was exactly the sort of house one would have expected him to live in and, years later, a frequent site for parties, to which, of course, I wouldn't go.

It occurred to me, however, as we pored over membranes, mitosis, and cells, that he was at heart the same guy, the same kid I'd eaten stale challah with on Sundays. "Yeah, well, I did what I could."

"Good for you," Zach said, glancing up from his textbook. One got the sense he was genuinely proud of me, as though he'd been rooting for me all along, and, though he could never sit beside me in biology, much less at lunchtime, there was at least a small, fledgling respect. We were also two Jews in a school that had somewhat few. "Can I tell you a secret?" he continued. (I shouldn't be repeating this but will.) "Tell me if this is normal. So Sandy"—Sandy was his golden retriever, who was currently lounging on a beanbag next to the desk—"she really likes peanut butter. I mean, she likes it a lot. So sometimes, you know, just for fun—"

The doorbell rang. It was Scott, our classmate, a youth hockey standout with flowing blond hair and Jared Leto-esque eyes. He and Zach had started a band of late, and he'd come for a practice at noon.

"Don't tell Scott, but sometimes, Sandy, she likes to lick peanut butter off me..."

I wasn't sure how to reply. Certainly, I'd seen strange things in my time. Even a kiss from Jill Brandt. And when you're in eighth grade, almost anything's possible. "Well, as long as she doesn't bite down—"

"She's got all these bumps on her tongue."

I looked down, stoically, at the grim, sleeping animal, who at every point trailed at his side.

"I'm just kidding about the licking," Zach said, though I wasn't sure that he was.

Soon Scott sauntered down, guitar at his side, his pony tail banded. "Wassup?" he said, grinning, then looked at me flustered, as if astonished that I was there.

~

In *The Origins of Totalitarianism,* Hannah Arendt, the German-Jewish philosopher, remarked that the "ideal subject of totalitarian rule is not the convinced Nazi or the convinced Communist, but people for whom the distinction between fact and fiction (i.e., the reality of experience) and the distinction between true and false (i.e., the standards of thought) no longer exist." What she meant by that is debatable, but it's part of her larger assertion that the first casualty of authoritarian rule, and perhaps the gravest one at that, is the loss of truth itself.

What made the middle school pecking order so attractive to all of us, logical even, is that it offered some semblance of truth. Zach Epstein indubitably belonged at the top, missed layups aside, precisely because he was so quick to the rim and, it would seem, the shorts of his comelier classmates. Whether one achievement fed off another is uncontested. Both were part of the same end. And that he would later turn out to be a fairly typical, domestic, aging, upper-class lawyer and, it was rumored, suppress his urge to come out, was irrelevant here. He was the king of our group. We needed him, in some sense. Needed to become him. He was everything that we sought. And one can't overlook the slow litany of terrors that is life in the middle school halls.

Thus, one can only imagine what it was like for the girls in our class to witness, as they did, come Tuesday morning, the day after the team tryouts, all of Erin Zoellick presenting her tray and sliding it down upon the Leaders' table, a crass intruder if there ever was. How she managed to insert herself was unclear. Even less clear was who had invited her—probably Paisley Essen, with whom she was rumored to be on good terms; it was also said they'd been caught smoking together, which was one of the surest ways in. Even more disturbing was the sight of Jill Brandt, her former best friend, and my latest accomplishment, as it were, having slid her cold tray further down, alone with the worst of them, moping, it seemed, near the back. Whether her best friend had just abandoned her, or whether she was disconsolate at having received a failed kiss this past summer, was probably less important than the way she stared at her plate—a blanched heap of spaghetti—while trying to feign interest in a conversation being made at her side.

A braver child than myself, a better one, in fact, would have talked to her then, would have slid my tray down next to hers—though boys and girls did not sit together, excluding a few queerer types—and I probably would have said something decent, something fitting and composed, as in, *I know we're probably never going to talk to each other again, or be friends, which is not to say we ever were, but I just wanted to thank you for having had me over this summer, and to tell you I like you a lot.* And that would be it. We would go our separate ways, and our eyes wouldn't meet with the hostility and frank awkwardness that would characterize our interactions for the next several years, as if we'd never been together, or our lips hadn't touched on that couch.

I didn't say any of these things, of course. I simply watched her with hands on my lap, also less interested in the food or budding social dynamics than the cruelty of life as it stood. The prior afternoon, during tryouts, I had embarrassed myself—missing several layups, stumbling into picks, scrambling around on defense—and I knew without hesitance that there was no way I was making that squad. Yet I wasn't a bad shooter—I could crank three's—and was about average height for my age. There was no reason I shouldn't make varsity, or sit with the Stars at the end.

I watched them now joking, munching on fries, their (mostly) shaven heads frizzy and hunched. Perhaps they were discussing Erin: how ugly she was, how she didn't belong in their sphere. Which, of course, everyone knew, even if it hadn't been said.

I sipped a root beer, digested my fries, then trundled upstairs to the gym. I had twenty minutes until French class began and thought I would practice my shot.

Already circling the rim was Roger Sherman, a fellow eighth-grader who had been new last year at the school. Roger, who was black, unlike almost everyone else in the school, lived nearly in Evanston and took a complex array of city buses to get to school. Being on scholarship (which none of us knew), he dressed uniformly in khakis and over-starched polos, rather than the ankle-length t-shirts and Girbaud jeans then in vogue—and wore enormous brown spectacles that even then didn't seem cool. He had memorized answers to *Jeopardy* and read dictionaries in his spare time. To say he'd never kissed a girl would be like saying that Erin Zoellick had never been felt up. One almost pitied him, and he was the closest thing I had to a friend.

We often shot hoops together or hung out until late, and he'd sometimes stay at my house, unless my parents chose to drive him, which they liked, inexplicably, to do. Later I would learn to attribute this to a residual sense—among both my parents and me—that we never quite felt at home among the WASP circles of Chicago Academy. In fact, I would later come to realize that the reason I'd transferred to the school in sixth grade is that I'd been denied admission in kindergarten for reasons that were never made clear, though, if one would guess, probably revolved around the fact that the school had enough upstart Jewish lawyers as parents. And Zach's mother was converted, and blonde.

"That tryout was bullshit," I muttered to Roger, who bounced me a pass at the arch.

"Same height for everyone," he said, referring to the rim, around which my shot clanked. He had also struggled at the tryouts, though, as always, he kept his nerve and threw up a medley of shots.

"Did you see who was sitting at the Leaders' table today?"

"Good for her," Roger smirked.

In high school, he and I would grow apart—right around the tenth grade, in fact, when he started befriending "higher" kids, namely Zach Epstein, and others with whom he played sports. For now, though, he was right at my level: new here, confused, fairly good at hoops, not overwhelming but decent enough to make squad.

"Who do you think's making it?"

"Heck if I know." Others had joined at this point, as we engaged in twenty-one. He popped his threes with aplomb. "Probably isn't me."

I guarded off, hanging back. "It should be," I added. "It should be both of us."

"Go tell that to the coach." He watched me a bit,

zestfully, biting his lip. Then he circled round to the rim.

~

In retrospect, I have to think Roger was kidding with the suggestion. But this was eighth grade, and it was hard to tell what was a joke. Besides, if Erin Zoellick could sit at the Leaders' table, there's no reason I, or Roger, for that matter, couldn't gain a spot on that team.

In truth, I recall very little about my youth. I remember, as I've mentioned, that Kiss. Or the smell of it, anyway. I remember the sheen of a suit, a teal double-breasted from Mark Shale in Northbrook that I wore to my Bar Mitzvah in December of 1991 (and where, of course, Zach Epstein had the first dance). And I remember above all the scented halls of my school, with its Aqua Net, Speed Stick, and Keds.

Most of all I remember three-twenty that day, when classes let out, and approximately twenty-one hours before the rosters for the teams would be announced—displayed on a white posterboard spanning the landing below the top floor. Presently, as others raced down the hall steps, anxious to get home, or wherever it was they unwound—the Leaders were rumored to smoke behind Mitchell's, a diner next to the school—I climbed the carpeted stairs, Roger Sherman trailing closely behind. He and I were intent on talking to the man, a fabled figure if there ever was.

Coach Musclebutt, as we called him, had to be approaching forty-five. A former college athlete who ran laps every morning around "the green" in Lincoln Park, he kept his head shaved and was short but solidly built. The girls all remarked on his ass, off of which, it was said, you could easily skip a small coin. He talked infrequently and, when obliged, spoke in the way that heavily muscled men will: as if the weight of words were too much for him, and too much for his own chiseled jaw.

"Can I help you?" he mumbled, as I knocked upon his

glass door.

His office looked out on the gym and the metal-fenced weight room, over which he seemed to preside. A fat stack of papers loomed on his desk, and trophies adorned the glass walls.

"Um, Coach, I was just wondering if me and Rodge could have a moment to talk with you. I don't mean to bother—"

"Come in," he grunted, turning to the mound of his desk.

Roger soon followed me, eyeing the display of brass.

We stood along the carpet, which smelled of raw Old Spice and several generations of sweat. "It's about the tryouts yesterday, Coach. I just wanted to say"—I eyed the floor, then somewhere in my heart found the will—"I just wanted to say that I think me and Rodge are good players. I mean, we're not the best in the class. But we try really hard. I mean, we care." That sounded *gay*, as I (woefully) would have said. In the cafeteria, talking like that could have gotten a boy maimed. "I mean, we care a lot about basketball, and we'll do whatever you say, and, well, I'm not sure if you've made the selection yet for the team, but I just wanted to say that I think if you put us on varsity, you wouldn't regret it, cause we could both contribute a lot." Yep, definitely *gay*. But I didn't know how else to explain it—how to articulate the fears that we felt.

Coach Musclebutt looked on confused, astounded, perhaps, that the two of us would have the audacity to enter his office and present our credentials like that. If he'd opted to punch us, I wouldn't have been surprised.

He sized up Roger then me. I, for my part, was now terrified, and Roger as if in a trance.

"So you two think *you* can play varsity?"

"Yes, sir," said Roger, then I.

About a decade later, I'd enlist in the Israeli Army. My memories of basic training, and of standing in formation for drill, begin with this encounter, with the sweat I would smell in this room.

"All right, I'll consider it," Coach Musclebutt grunted in what was probably the loudest voice he could make. "Dismissed." He might not have said *dismissed*. That might have been my Platoon Sergeant. As I said, the memories begin to overlap.

Racing down the hall steps, Roger said nothing.

"You wanna come for dinner?" I asked. "I think my mom's making brisket."

"Why not?"

I didn't sleep that night, and neither did he. Like many a night after, Roger camped out in a sleeping bag next to my bed. We stayed up late watching *Night Court* and *Cheers* and then the blurry images of the adult channels that were viciously blocked.

Dawn found us weary-eyed, beyond the point of nervous, with no homework done, our teeth raw. Roger often brought a change of clothes with him, though he hadn't this time. The high-waisted blue jeans and neon Agassi tennis shirt didn't exactly suit him, and he cut a strange image in school, though he didn't seem to mind, and neither did I, as our only focus that day was the sheet going up after twelve.

I remember little of that morning—not the quiz I'd bungled on cytosis; nor the disagreements between Booker T. Washington and W. E. B. Du Bois; nor even the deeper meaning of *Things Fall Apart* ("A man who calls his kinsmen to a feast does not do so to save them from starving," wrote Chinua Achebe, about which I might well have taken heed). Rather, all I recall was the look on Jill Brandt's face as we emerged from Algebra, as if she knew something about which I'd be keen. It wasn't a puzzled looked exactly, more like a placid one, as if the truth itself had been affirmed. Perhaps Bill Clinton had been elected, the Pope's picture torn up, or Erin Zoellick cut down to size. Jill gripped her binder and started towards the hall, still casting that ponderous grin.

No, I wouldn't kiss her, not then, nor again. I'm not even sure I once did.

But I remember the moment when I saw that white sheet, which was plastered along the stairs hall, and the way the names were printed in a gummy dot matrix: Epstein, then Sherman, then . . . *me*.

I couldn't believe it. My tiny heart sank. I nearly fell off the stairs. Other kids passed me, pawed at the sheet. "All of that's bullshit," one said. Others could believe it. I didn't care. All I knew is that from that moment—and for the rest of my life—Roger and I would always have something to prove.

Pink Bed

Little would like to climb down from her perch on the
toilet seat but she must wait. She's hungry and her mouth
tastes like fuzz and sour milk. Listening, she can tell there
are at least two women in the ladies' room. One in a stall
talking to her friend about what a good idea it was to come
early and beat the crowds, and the other at the sink saying
technology has ruined the world. There might be a third
woman, it's hard to tell. There are ones who come in and
she doesn't know they are there until she is startled by
a flushing toilet. Little wants them to shut up and leave.
Her legs are asleep and don't even feel like legs anymore,
but she cannot punch them awake. She cannot move until
these women leave and let her climb off the toilet and crawl
under the door. Right now her bottom is wedged far enough
back so each sneakered foot can take a space on the end of
the U-shaped lid. Cold metal pipes dig into her spine. She
knows there will be a leftover damp spot on the back of her
light blue sweatshirt from the metal sweat. She wishes the
toilet had a lid like the one at home. It would make keeping
her feet off the floor so much easier.

It's a tricky business, that's what her mom would say if
she was here. She talks about everything like that, a tricky
business but don't worry, kiddo, we'll pull it off. Yes, this
getting out of the bathroom stall is a tricky business, but
Little will pull it off. Yesterday she waited too long and
the bathroom door never stopped swinging open. It took
forever all the women on line to finish using the other toilet
stall. Little's stall, the one with the sign her mom placed
there, *Toilet broken*, made a lot of people complain, and

Little had sat inside, cold and damp and thinking about how her mom said the most important thing is to never let anyone notice you. Little had to blend in like wallpaper, like paint. Her mom had shown her, pressed against the wall, and said, *Freeze like this, see? You can't even see me, I am still like paint,* and it had made Little laugh.

It wasn't as funny now, being still like paint, but she won't move. She remembers how mom said someone would grab her if she was seen crawling from underneath a broken stall door, a kid alone.

The woman by the sink is complaining that she has pumped soap into her hand but cannot get the water to come out at the sink. "What was wrong with the old faucets anyway? At least you could get the damn water to come out. Jeannie, help me, I've got soap in my hands and no water." Little would like to tell the woman how to do it, to hold her hand low under the faucet to make the hidden button push out water, but she knows better.

Little hears the other woman laugh and then the sound of running water. She can't see them because of the paper she taped to the crack in the door after she saw eyes staring in at her, a little kid who tried to tell her mom that someone was in there but her mother told her to mind her own business. Little found the paper that night, beige packing paper in the shelves under the cash register for wrapping breakable objects. She took sheets of it, and tape, and a half-full tin of mints. She is not supposed to take things but she told herself it was okay, she needed to stay hidden, and she was only borrowing.

The tape is in her aqua and orange backpack—which she also took, from the back-to-school display. So is the tin, but she ate all the mints. She feels bad about the mints. She can't give them back since she ate them, so that makes it stealing. The backpack is only borrowing. When her mom comes back and offers her a present for being good, Little will ask for the backpack so she can have it when she starts first grade in the fall. That should be soon, she thinks. She thinks about Miss Connie, her kindergarten teacher, and how she gave her extras at snack time and told her she was a good artist. Little stops thinking about her because it makes her feel sad.

Come today, she tells her mom in her head. *Come today or I will make Miss Connie my mom. My new mom. Maybe I will love her best. You don't know. You'd better come today.*

Little remembers the way her mom smelled when she leaned in to tell her to be brave, like cigarettes, like oranges from their favorite soap.

Just a day or two, her mom had said, *just to get this new thing started up. It's safer than at home because of that nosy neighbor who wants to get us thrown out. It's not like you will be alone, there is always someone at the store. But you have to be good. If you don't stay hidden, you will get us both in trouble and they will take you away from me forever. Just a few days. You can be my helper, Little Bit.*

The dull small roar of the hot air hand blower, the women's voices getting fainter the door closes after them.

Little punches her legs and moves them off the toilet. It's okay that she falls, she has to be on the floor anyway to crawl like a crab sideways under the stall door. She stands up, wobbly, just in time. The door opens again and it's a woman in a red sweater helping a white-haired older woman with a walker. They are busy trying to keep the door from closing on them, since they are moving so slowly, and they don't even look up as Little scoots past them into the hallway with the water fountain. Little drinks until her stomach sloshes, but she is still hungry.

The store is busy—good, that makes things so much easier. She wonders if it is the weekend. When she came with Mom during work hours, it was always easier to not get noticed on the weekend. But then they would go home and Little did not have to worry about filling her growling tummy. Yesterday she found a piece of cake on a table in the restaurant, just a few bites missing. She ate it until she thought someone was looking at her, and then she hid herself in the crowd, licking the icing off her fingers. Thinking about this makes her hungrier even though she ate a stolen banana and a pack of cookies before she went to sleep. If her mom does not come today, Little will have to say more *Sorrys* later, before she can sleep. Sorry for stealing. Sorry for leaving the hiding place in the bathroom. Sorry for thinking mean thoughts about her mom because she hasn't come back yet. When her mom shows up, Little is going to ask for cake with chocolate icing and pink icing roses because she has been so good and it has been too long.

Little feels her eyes stinging with tears. She squints so they will not spill out. Crying makes people look. Her mom almost got fired when someone saw Little crying just weeks ago, and they called about a lost child on the intercom, and they said her mom shouldn't have brought her kid to work even if it was just one time because the babysitter didn't show. They didn't know there was no babysitter. They didn't know it had been lots of times.

Little takes the escalator up to the fourth level, tagging behind a family so she looks like she belongs. She loves the fourth level. Not only does she blend in because it's the kids' section and there are always a lot of kids running around and no one notices who is with who, but because it is fun to play with all the toys. Little stays near the family until she can drift away toward her favorite toy, the big dollhouse with six rooms, three up and three down, full of tiny furniture and teeny tiny plates and a flowerpot in the window, even a little dog and cat. She finds her favorite doll, with long brown hair like her own, and she puts her at the table and serves her pretend pancakes on little tiny plates. Her doll wants orange juice. Little pours a pretend glass. She lets the cat sit on the table and eat out of a bowl for company. If Little had a cat she would let her sit on the table, too. They would have their own room and a dollhouse just like this and her cat would have its own toy cat to play with. She lets her doll have second helpings of pancakes. When her doll is full and sleepy, she gets to pick which bed she wants to take a nap in: the one with the blue quilt with polka dots. Her doll is falling asleep when a girl from the family Little followed up is by her side, watching. She is smaller than Little, maybe only four, and she wants to play so Little hands her one of the other dolls, one with hair like fluff.

Their dolls make cookies in the kitchen. Little can almost taste the peanut butter ones when she says the words on her tongue, but her new friend says she is allergic to nuts so they agree to make chocolate chip. There are bowls and pots in the dollhouse kitchen and Little and her friend pretend there is batter inside of them and lick pretend cookie dough off pretend spoons. When her friend's mom looks up from fussing over her baby in a stroller and says, "Time to go!", Little trails after them, keeping a slight distance, watching the mom coo at the baby and then smile at her little girl. Ahead is another mom, yelling at three boys who are throwing the kids' pillows with dinosaur shapes on them. Little is glad to see the sales clerk at the nearby desk staring at them, not at her. The family she is trailing stop at the elevator. Little can't join them. Everyone notices you in an elevator.

Little is warm and pulls her sweatshirt over her head. The static makes her long brown hair go all electric and she giggles. Her pink t-shirt has a tomato stain on it from pizza a few days ago. Her pants are sticky from where she wiped her hands off on them after eating what she could find in the garbage cans by the restaurant cafe before they were emptied. She can imagine how her mom will pretend to be shocked, using a silly, fakey voice, *You mean you actually want a bath?* Her mom can be really funny when she isn't mad or sad or really, really tired. Little is thinking about her mom inside her head and doesn't notice the saleswoman in front of her until it is too late.

"Excuse me, are you lost? Do you need help finding your family?" She has a nice smile. She is younger than mom, the kind her mom growls about, saying the teenagers and college kids are stealing all the jobs. Little points to a woman standing next to a stroller a few aisles to the left and forces herself to skip over to the stroller. The woman is turning a green ceramic bowl over in her hand to look at the price tag on the bottom. She is darker than Little, and Little is worried the salesgirl will not believe they are family. She rests her hand on the push bar and looks at the saleswoman who smiles and turns away. Inside the stroller, a fat baby with a thatch of black hair looks up at Little with a blank expression and makes a bird sound. Little drops her hand off the bar and steps away as the mom turns to smile at her baby. The saleswoman is not looking anymore, but is too near the escalators for Little to go down, so she sneaks over to the stairwell, hunger pulling her to the second floor. She passes a young man smoking on the third floor stairwell, who almost grinds out his cigarette but then relaxes when he sees it is just a kid. She skips past him, tense that she will feel a hand on her arm and she will be caught, but he is back on his phone again, his cigarette dangling from his mouth.

The store has gotten very crowded. The restaurant is packed. She spies the family of her new friend eating in the back. The mom and the rough boys are two tables over. One of the boys has shoved a French fry up each nostril and is getting yelled at while his brothers laugh. Little tells herself to avoid that table for leftovers.

Oh, lucky, two women and their children are leaving. Little slides behind them as they strap the younger two kids in strollers and tell the other kids to come along. A boy with a ketchup-stained face looks back at her as she slides his uneaten chicken nuggets into her hand. "Momma," he howls, "She took my nuggies," but Little is gone, and one of the two nuggets are already in her mouth. There is a half carton of milk on another table, and a half slice of pizza sitting on a tray.

She goes from level to level all day, mixing in and out of the crowd until she feels she cannot walk anymore. She follows an old man and his wife up to the fourth floor on the escalator. She watches the door of her bathroom until it looks all clear and she can slip inside and under her locked stall door. She has to stay there very quiet in case the custodian comes in and swabs down the floor with his mop. She keeps her nose hidden in her hands as the ammonia tang hits her nose, as the mop sliding under the door freezes her with fear. Yesterday someone jiggled the door handle after the custodian left, muttered how they don't fix nothing in this goddam store. But tonight, no one comes.

The store closes. In an hour or two the lights will go out on the main floors, and go dim in the stairwells. The exit sign of the bathroom stays on. Little tells herself not to be scared, as she has every night this last long sleepover. She is safer than she would be home alone—that's what her mom said. Besides, it is easier to move around when the lights are out.

When it's been dark for a long time, Little leaves the bathroom and sticks to the stairwell, her fingers tracing the concrete walls in the dimmed light as she listens for the security guard. He goes floor to floor, swinging his flashlight, talking to someone on his phone or sitting on a chair in a corner dozing, his hat down over his eyes.

She makes her way back up to the fourth floor where the children's furniture is. She visits the pink bed to say the important thing. In the princess bedroom with the unicorn pillows with the ruffled edges and the pink netting with fat fabric flowers, she climbs into the pink bed and smooths the comforter nicely in place. Under the covers, she can look up at where fabric flowers fasten pink netting to all four posts, and she lets her hair spread out on the fancy pillows just like a real princess.

At home, she sleeps on the couch that smells like old washcloths and peanut butter. Her mom stays up late, sometimes talking to herself, sometimes singing, sometimes crying. Little's last night there, her mom woke her up in the middle of the night and said, *Dance with me, Little,* and took Mr. Stripey Tiger in her arms and danced around the room. Little was too sleepy to dance but it was funny until her mom was yelling the song words too loud and jumping on the couch and the neighbor came *bang bang bang* on the door, *Shut up in there you crazy bitch.* That old neighbor is that bad word, Little thinks, not her mom.

She misses her mom so very hard. She whispers that to the fabric flowers out loud so her mom can hear. This is a magic bed, she knew it the first time she saw it, and she knows this is the place where her wish can be heard. She'd been sure her mother would come today but now she knows it is too late. It will have to be tomorrow. Her mom will make her a room like this in a brand new apartment with money from the new job she told Little she was getting. There will be cake at night, chocolate and pink frosting roses. She will say, *I am sorry I took so long to come back,* and Little will say, *It is all right, Mommy,* and there will be a warm bath. She will fall asleep listening to sound of her mother singing.

Little touches her fingertips together three times to make the wish come true, and then she must leave the pink bed. The guard must not catch her in it.

Up the steps, her fingers tracing the concrete walls, she listens again for the security guard. In the far back of the fifth floor, she crawls into the lowest long shelf where rolled rugs are stacked like big fat fingers. She finds the quilt she has tucked behind the rugs on a low shelf and wraps herself tightly. She can just make out the safety lights twinkling like stars on the ceiling across the long room, and an exit sign over a door holding its steady red glowing promise as she closes her eyes. She can say her *Sorrys* now, before she falls asleep, including her sorry for not staying all night in the bathroom like her mom said to do. After the first night, when she fell off the toilet and hit her head, she has been sleeping behind the rugs and sneaking back into the bathroom when the workers come in, staying there until the store is safely filled with people. She will explain this to her mom tomorrow. And her mom will not get mad because it has been too long, and her mom is the one who needs to say a sorry.

The noise wakes her in the morning, the vacuum growl too close to her. She has slept too long. She has to sneak low and quiet behind the vacuum noise and the back of the woman pushing it. That was a close one. She will tell her mom sorry today, she was right, she should have stayed in her bathroom stall as she'd been told.

There is a woman inside Little's bathroom. Her back is to Little. She is tearing down all the paper taped inside Lil's stall door and saying, "What the hell?" When she steps out holding the aqua and orange backpack, all Little can do is stare for a moment.

She recognizes the woman in the same moment the woman turns and recognizes her— someone her mom asked to watch her once when they were having a break and eating, and the woman said, *No, I am sorry,* and *You can't keep bringing her here or they will have your ass fired,* but now she is looking at Little and down at the backpack and she says, "Oh, no. God, no, she didn't."

Little turns and runs out the door. She doesn't have to look back to know she is being chased, but she knows this store better than anyone else and soon the woman's yelling voice fades. *Security to fourth floor,* she hears the loudspeaker order, but she is through the door to the stairs already. She runs all the way to the first. The doors just opening and the early bird shoppers are surging in. She feels eyes on her as she runs towards the doors, a crackle in the air, and she pushes through the wave of incoming people and out the doors into the parking lot. The sun is like a slap to her face, surprising her after the long cool of the store. Cars sit row after row, like metal fish in an endless sea, sun glinting off the metal roofs and glass windshields, sending sparks of light to dazzle her eyes. Little knows she has to move away from the mouth of the doors, they will open again any minute and arms will try to catch her. Where to go, which way to go, there is no choice but just go, to follow her feet whichever way they are running.

A. Molotkov

Destination

"I'm really hungry," Goombeldt said as they walked onto the platform.

"Can't you wait till we get there?" Zungvilda's voice was tense, as if she was prepared but unwilling to fight.

"Are you joking? It's almost five hours."

The train's small face had already appeared in the distance; they could hear its tired rumble. The gray platform lay there, impersonal, identical to every other platform in the world, hot and sticky on this summer day. The neat, predictable station building perched next, its dark brown the color of defeat—the truest color. They had just gotten here, and yet, Goombeldt was already tired of this town. He couldn't wait to move on.

The train pulled up with its slowing rhythm of wheels.

"Maybe they will have some food on the train," Zungvilda offered mechanically, without fully believing herself.

"I doubt it. Not here."

"Then go get something to eat." Zungvilda attempted to preserve an even tone.

"Great. Do you want to come?"

"No, I'll wait for you on the train. Let's get our bags in first, if you don't mind."

"Good idea." Now that Zungvilda had backed off, Goombeldt knew he too should make an effort and act with kindness. This trip was supposed to be fun. No point in starting it with an argument.

The train opened up and sat there, patient and available, its cars identical, its blue and white horizontal lines disappearing into the distance. Just a few passengers populated its vast worm body. Goombeldt and Zungvilda carried their luggage inside: two identical pieces, dark-green, imbued with protective rectangular intention.

Their compartment was just a few doors down. It looked comfortable but shabby, the way things get where it costs less to keep them up forever than to invest in a replacement.

Goombeldt left the suitcases on the floor and headed to the station in search of something edible. His digestive system was in the middle of an extended hungry symphony.

But the building was utterly devoid of food. Unbelievable, at a large train station! Something of this sort could be possible only in a sleepy, backward place like this, untouched by progress. Goombeldt was ready to get out of here, excited about their ultimate destination. (You knew how misguided this was.) He consulted his watch. Thirteen minutes until departure. He still had time to look around. He crossed the gloomy hall, its benches brown like the building itself, its floor fake marble gray. He was tempted to run yet restrained by some misplaced notion of dignity, resulting in an exaggeratedly fast gait.

Zungvilda stayed in her seat, looking out the window, her hands in front of her on the foldout table, next to a magazine she had gotten out of her purse but not opened. The station offered very little visual information. With barely any passengers, the place seemed frozen in time, a forgotten intersection invented by the two of them. Why had they chosen to start here? Everyone insisted that a trip like this was exactly what was needed to fix their relationship. Once they stepped outside their dull everydays, the boredom of their lives was supposed to dissolve, making room for a new interpretation of what being together meant for the two of them.

A small café with its neon lights still on perched across

the station square. The door stood open. Goombeldt was excited, vindicated. Walking very fast, he crossed the square and entered. He checked his watch again. Nine more minutes. There seemed to be no one inside. The sign by the cash register said *Wait to be seated*. Goombeldt stood there for a minute, uneasy, hoping for someone to show up and resolve his predicament. He strained his ears for signs of human presence. Nothing but the ticking of the clock on the opposite wall. No remote conversation in the back room, not even the sound of running water in the kitchen. Yet, somebody had to be there. It was unlikely that everyone had just walked off, leaving the door wide open. (If Goombeldt had checked inside the kitchen, he would have seen you crouching behind the sink, acutely aware of the passage of time. But he didn't check.)

Zungvilda consulted her watch. Eight minutes. Goombeldt had better hurry up if he didn't want to miss the train. She wondered what could be keeping him so long. This was so much like him—placing a momentary whim over her peace of mind, over their shared plans. After all, she had suggested they bring some snacks from the hotel, but Goombeldt had discarded her suggestion. He was tired of the hotel's menu and wanted to pick up something different at the station. How could he be tired so soon? They had just arrived the night before and had only one meal there.

She imagined him chatting to a hot dog vendor, indifferent to the possibility that she might be worried—in fact, enjoying it. He would probably return two minutes before the departure, flaunting his punctuality and his precise mastery over time as if it were a magic gift rather than the nuisance she considered it.

She opened the magazine and tried to read, but the words did not reach her mind.

Goombeldt looked at his watch—only seven minutes remained. He knew he needed at least three or four to walk back to the train. If he ran, he could make it in two.

"Anyone here?" he said loudly.

(You had no intention of responding.)

"Anyone?" Goombeldt shouted, a note of desperation in his voice. "Hello!" The green tablecloths, the folded napkins, the dimmed lights—all of these things seemed to be in on a secret. (Perhaps you smiled precisely at that moment.)

Zungvilda checked the time. Only five minutes. An announcement over the loudspeaker concurred. Where in the world was he? All at once, it became obvious to her that this whole plan, this trip, the entire notion that it would cure their relationship, was a mere illusion. And she didn't feel surprised. It was too late. They had squandered away their mutual affection. They barely cared about each other anymore, not in any real sense. All they cared about was the routine of their life, the investment of their relationship, the effort they had expended to maintain it through twelve years as a couple. Now she knew: this rejuvenation trip was nothing but an extended farewell.

Goombeldt checked the time. Just four minutes. He was cutting it dangerously close. He rushed into the kitchen, looked around. No one; no food in view. Goombeldt knew he had to give up.

Zungvilda frowned. Three minutes. Perhaps he had decided to stay behind, to send her off all by herself as a punishment for whatever she might have done wrong, in his opinion. She would not have any of it! Abruptly, she abandoned her seat and walked out.

On the platform, she looked around, but Goombeldt was nowhere to be seen.

"We are about to depart," the conductor confided to Zungvilda. His black uniform was old, patched up on one side, discolored around the armpits. His face was sad, unhealthy, his expression gloomy and detached.

"I know. But my husband is not back yet. What should I do?"

"We can't delay the departure. Maybe he changed his mind?"

"He couldn't have changed his mind!" Zungvilda cried. She ran towards the station.

Just at that moment, Goombeldt emerged on the platform. He had taken a shortcut around the station building instead of going through it. It was first like a dream, and then not a dream at all, that he saw the train's tail come into motion two minutes early. He was about to sprint in order to jump into the last car when he saw Zungvilda running away from him, entering the station.

"Wait!" he yelled, but she was inside before she could hear him. She hadn't noticed the premature departure. Or perhaps she'd just ignored it. Something like that could be expected from Zungvilda.

He ran towards the station, the platform's gray hopeless under his feet. Out of breath—even after so short a run— he pushed the heavy door, hoping to get her attention immediately. But she had already disappeared from sight, perhaps looking for him in one of the side sections, or even in the station square he had left a minute ago. Through the closing door, he saw the accelerating train pass the end of the platform.

At least we both stayed behind, Goombeldt thought with relief as he scanned the station. He knew Zungvilda was near. And there she was, hesitant, nearly but not quite facing him, yet failing to notice him. He approached.

"Why did you get off?" His voice was tense, the balance of guilt between the two of them still tenuous.

"I was looking for you. Where have you been?"

"Trying to get something to eat, where else?"

"You missed the train in the meantime." Zungvilda's voice was scornful.

"I wouldn't have missed the train if you hadn't run off on me. I was ready to get on when I saw you entering the station."

"How was I supposed to know that? I wasn't about to get stuck on that train all by myself. This whole trip was your idea anyway!"

"Was it? I thought this was something we both wanted to do." Goombeldt's voice had turned sad, detached.

"No need to try to blame it all on me. Next time just get your meal before you leave the hotel." Zungvilda's irritation was clear. Her face reddened. The two or three people inside the station observed them without appearing to do so.

"But you . . ." Goombeldt halted, his anger instantly replaced by worry. "What about our luggage? Did you get it out?"

"No. How could I?"

"So you just hopped off that train and left it all behind?"

"Exactly," she replied with irony of her own, grinning at his self-satisfied face, staring him down.

"But all of our things are there. Our passports. And most of our money too."

"I guess we'll have to telegraph the destination and ask them to hold it for us."

"Have you forgotten where we are? They will split the money and tell us the suitcases were stolen on the way."

"What else can we do?" Zungvilda felt as if this scene was happening to someone else, as if a solution had already been provided and they just didn't know it yet. Then, shaking off her indifference, she answered her own question: "We must catch up with the train and grab our things before someone else gets hold of them."

"How will we do that?"

"We must run very fast," Zungvilda returned with a dark spark in her eyes. "We'll rent a car, of course."

"Here?"

"There should be a car rental around here, shouldn't there?"

"I suppose so."

Zungvilda felt a strange, misplaced sense of relief at the thought that they had missed their train, however absurd this might have been, considering that it had taken away everything they'd had with them. The loss had birthed this new plan in her head; forward progress was bound to continue, and she was in the leading role.

They reentered the train station. Predictably, the Information booth was deserted, the attendant's office chair pushed all the way back, away from the service window. Crumpled paper balls littered the floor, as if the attendant was a hesitant poet.

They had to find the car rental on their own. They walked fast, almost ran through the station into the square, scrutinizing the area, holding hands, happy to have a goal, increasingly intoxicated by this forced adventure.

Miraculously, a rental office awaited in a nearby street. They rushed in, happy, as if they were young again. A modest selection of vehicles welcomed them. Their streak of bad luck was over.

"We are in a rush," Goombeldt said to the rental clerk. "Can you please hurry? There is a good tip in it for you." He was relieved that at least his wallet was still in his pocket.

"Sure thing," the clerk confirmed.

Indeed, the paperwork was minimal—a brief, faded form—and just a few minutes later they were ready to go. Goombeldt asked for directions, tipped the attendant. Tipping was something he excelled at.

He volunteered to drive, and they were on their way. The car felt small, uncomfortable, its beige seats exuding a chemical scent signaling an overuse of detergent.

"The whole train ride was supposed to be four and a half hours, and we are about fifteen minutes behind," Zungvilda said. "The train doesn't stop between here and there. We'll have to go really fast."

"Sure."

The freeway, the car flying to catch up with the hope of the train—all of this felt strange, as if they were trying too hard to fix something that had outlived its usefulness. But strangely, it felt real, an objective predicament, not something planned. For the first time since they had left home, Zungvilda was truly involved. Goombeldt focused on the road ahead, his foot steady on the gas, the freeway almost empty, so empty there was no reason why they wouldn't be able to catch up, going as fast as they were. No reason at all.

"I'm sorry," Zungvilda said.

She did feel sorry. However annoyed she might have been at Goombeldt from time to time, she realized she was at last comfortable with him in this adventure, content to think of her life with him in it.

"Sorry about what?"

She didn't really know. "Sorry about getting off the train like that."

"It was my fault. You were right. I should have brought some food from the hotel. It was stupid of me."

His own determination of an hour ago now seemed ridiculous. Had he followed her advice, they would be on the train, perfectly comfortable, relaxing, enjoying each other's company. Sometimes he hated himself for his inability to stop in time, before his actions caused irreversible damage. Once wound up, he found it hard to unwind. But it was always a reaction to something Zungvilda had done. Always cause and effect—underneath all the balancing, the joy of their life together had faded, and he was truly sorry.

"You were tired of the hotel food," Zungvilda reminded softly.

"Yes, I was. But that's no reason to miss the train."

Both were silent for a while.

"I love you," she finally said, digging deep into herself to verify this.

"I love you too." He glanced at her quickly, his brown eyes the same as they had always been since they'd met: large, inquisitive, capable of attention.

The freeway rushed by, surreal in the early evening light, nearly abandoned, as if there was no need to go anywhere today, as if all attempts to move in space were futile. Zungvilda closed her eyes for a moment. The tenderness she had just expressed remained with her. She knew that when they got to their destination, the craze of their bizarre vacation would once again catch up with them, wrap them up, drag them along. She opened her eyes. Once the vacation was over, they would have no new lives awaiting them, just their own two lives mixed up together.

Something was blocking the lane ahead. They got closer. It was a car, stopped in the middle of their lane. The driver must have stepped out for a minute—to use the bathroom, to stretch, to take a few pictures. Indeed, the view was beautiful: a distant mountain range presiding over a green spread of fields. But why leave the car in the middle of the lane like that, even on a near-deserted freeway?

(Only you knew.)

Goombeldt had to use the opposing lane to bypass the stopped car—there was a truck coming, but it was at least a hundred yards away, and he had enough time to make it. He would hate to wait for that slow truck.

But then, mid-move, the car already in the opposing lane, Goombeldt pressing his foot all the way down, he remembered: this was a rental—it could not accelerate as quickly as his own car—it struggled, hesitated to change gears. There was a long moment when Goombeldt and Zungvilda both wondered—and then the truck was upon them, traveling faster than Goombeldt had calculated. He made a mad tug at the wheel just as he cleared the stopped car on his right—but too late, not enough space. The truck's broad face clipped the driver's side of their rental. The sound was deafening. Their vehicle spun out of control, slid off the road, but remained upright and the air bags did not deploy.

Zungvilda's seatbelt kept her in her seat. The truck honked three times and sped up on its way as if nothing had happened.

She looked to her left. She knew immediately; she had already known Goombeldt was dead, from the way the truck had hit the car, from the red splashes on the dashboard. She turned away. She felt strangely calm. Not counting the likely bruising from the seatbelt, she was unharmed. Shards of glass from the windshield were everywhere, even in her hair. She had imagined a life without Goombeldt so many times, even longed for it—but now, those images felt immaterial. She would have to find out what her own life really was.

Zungvilda sat there for a while. Then she opened the door, got out. She had to catch a ride to the nearest rest stop to call the police. She remembered having just passed a small town. She remained calm, detached. She saw a car approaching and stood in the middle of the lane so that the driver would see her right away.

(Traveling fast, you giggled when her figure moved into view.)

As the car got close, it slowed down a bit, and Zungvilda remained in the middle of the lane, expecting the driver to stop.

(But you pressed gas instead.)

ALEC MONTALVO

PASSERSBY IN THE TRAINYARD

the tallied moments lost between each blink becomes
the drifter   the circling tourist atop a platform their
thumb out   nursing maps   maybe caught on a stairwell
     in bedrooms   sometimes fornicated   throughout
door frames   passing through subway station turnstiles
between the train cars   maybe all the way up to
the moon   a moon that blinks between the turn of each
month   within each moon blink   rain   under rain
i become a boy kicking doorknobs down the avenue
i collect the fleeting junk caught above the grates
a drainpipe guarding the basin   of mutually collected
throwaways   caged ceilings for sidewalks   after
everything has passed   I slip under there with the
crocodiles
     fashion gauntlets   from the teeth of ex-lovers
blinked   i banquo into the dinner parties   blink slept
throughout the turnstile moon cycle   finger in pocket
     pulled it out like a pocket watch and when you asked me
which train to take to get to the city   you asked me between
all the blinks   all the eyes all the eyes all the eyes
     i blinked in your eyes   for the first time

GABRIEL MUNDO
AN OVERHEARD CONVERSATION

Ay, qué lástima por Monica. They tell you, come to this country,
you'll have a better life, and then, como magia, you lose a
daughter.
Te digo, I don't know how she's here right now. I pray
for her every night. Oye, are you listening?   Only in America,
te digo. Uncle Sam sees some brown skin and says, tómalo!
And once you take it, then what? You go back to work wiping
tables and scrubbing toilets.   Madre mia, what a week.
And I know I couldn't make it to the wake but believe me
I was praying harder than anyone else.   No, no,
I was in town, but I had a birthday party to go to.
Well, anyways, what about her kids? Pobrecitos. Te digo,
if they were in front of me, I would never let them go.
They're good kids, you know. I met them once. Hold on, wait,
here she comes.

                                    Gracias.
Madre mia, madre mia, I almost started crying. She looks terrible,
like she's the one who took the bullet.   No, I didn't
mean it like that!   She just looks like she needs
a break. I mean how long was she gone? A week, maybe two?
            Te digo, I've known her since she first got here
so don't start accusing me of things.   Bueno. Anyways, I'm
about done. Are you?   Pues, should we go?
        Mierda! Do you have any cash for the tip?
Yes? Oh, bless you. Te digo, I don't know what I'd do without you.

Lot's Wife (I)

Nothing was there to warn me about me.
No blaring trumpets, no glaring specters
foretold my best intentions were no more
than puny wicks consumed in desire.
The tragedy of yearning was always
there, like a weed, underestimated.
How could I know a love of forbidden
nested inside me, that it would wake one
night, hungry, soar, wings out to here,
eyes wide, wild, hunting for some small heartbeat
to deliver me from thinness? What was
it, an acre away from paradise,
what vine of memory grabbed me, made me
look back, as salt poured into my grieving?

ROSE MARIA WOODSON
LOT'S WIFE (II)

You never heard my silence. You never
heard the simmering fission of ego
splitting into asterisk & fury.
My name became mere chaff, moral punchline
blown away in a cautionary tale,
my loss, broken-bone deep, dismissed weakness
for all time. Even when I was with you
I hovered elsewhere, overlooked, in blue
horizons you never saw. You heard rain,
you heard wind, you heard sparrows. You never
heard the narrowing of my plunged heart. When
did you notice I was no longer with
you, as I tried to glean roses from ash,
glancing one last time through my own window.

Heather Quinn
A Certain Light

how her eyes reflected that small square window as she
studied
> clouds
>> marbled light of dawn

concentration of blue kernel, rain permeating the burn

he tasted of tannins, olive oil the first time they kissed

>> she tasted of fermented yeast
scent of bread baking

the way her skin gave off radiant heat
> *friction* is what he thought

she should have come of age in the 1920s or 40s

> wearing flapper dresses to speakeasies

> overalls for building B-52 bombers

he remembers dim table lamps casting her silhouette
against the restaurant's far wall

how she lit a cigarette

flecks of ash like flurries in her hair [black as ravens]

how lowlights reflected sequins as she danced

burst of flame from her welding torch

she loved black and white film, imagined Lena Horne

lips painted scarlet as she walked onscreen for the first time

[luminous red]

will they say death raised shadows as she let loose her last
breath or maybe it was a star
flew from her lips

once in mid-night, they snuck into the backyard to make
snow angels

she could not stifle her giggles

he said to *hush*
waking everyone would ruin the moonlight

ANNA SEIDEL

SOFT AS BLUE IN QUESTIONING HANDS

The search for what's next makes honey clump. A
meandering dream on prey.

Pupils in the garden of anagrams.
Do you wake me with a mirror image from my next dream?

I whispered my name,
in the hope it'd stop the questioning.

Will you lure my unheard heart from its cage?

Anna Seidel

Swallow our playful book before it sings

Snow will fall. I will have
walked on legs of ink. No longer a place to seek.

Everything will be re-named. She'd only given me minutes;
so, to maybe fall asleep.
It's a tipping point.

As if I had composed a symphony from noises
and as if my hands were dipped in honeycombs.
I could write, but no creature wanted to fit its given name.

Too little did these ideas seem to distinguish themselves
from lying.
Suddenly, it's too bright to cast another magic spell.

A warming gold will poison my heart
in the garden where nothing was ever meant to grow.

Norman Walter

Radio Silence

Life seems to be more happening the
day after it rains

in the city, and old folks is sweeping
their cat stoops and sidewalks
loose leaves litter the cobble-cracked roads
and never-ending crooked alleyways,

the bee-bop bustle of bike riders, pedestrian
foot-traffic, the cars strolling by, and dogs
barking back in response to it all,

street sweepers swoosh the slush of
leaves and fresh rain waters down
city gutters,
vacant scraps of fragmented light
surrender unto and gleam against
alleyway walls peering between the
geometrical gaps and spaces of homes
and much taller buildings,

splashing the spillage of light
across evening hours, and neighbors pass
on their way to yoga, walking dogs,
coming back home from the
grocery around the corner, and
coming home to their loved ones,

and here I am,
feeling as though I've danced
madly within a disco
without hearing the music,
without feeling the heat or push of bodies,
shoved into a solitary corner
fatigued and formless, and without
seeing the beauty in any of it.

Special section
SANCTUARY

Tina M. Johnson

Complications

> After watching *4.1 Miles*, a documentary about
> European migrants crossing the Aegean Sea.

What you want, a simple thing:
let this child be left alone to live her life,
but you know the world is bound to break her

because somewhere people are leaving their homes,
crossing landscapes of water like mountain ranges,
holding onto nothing but locked fingers.

You know how things happen in this world, even
if they haven't happened to you—

dogs snap at the throats of children,
hands turn white in the water,
a man reaches down into the ocean sixty times,
one hundred,
until the deck of his boat is gasping with people.

That night he will lie awake in the dark, eyes wide as a doe's,
counting their faces, trying to prove to himself
that no one was left behind, that finally
the ocean was as empty as a doorway.

Imagine now, my granddaughter, small as an eggplant,
turning and kicking inside the warm salt of her mother's
womb.
Impossible to believe she lives in the same world
with the child who rides the dolorous slab of boat,
whose mother lifts the crown
of her head above water,
a little queen fighting to breathe in a new country.

What you want are simple things:
a child tucked into bed,
a mother unafraid of water,
a man peaceful in his mind.

You want
the world to stop spinning the way it is spinning now,
to pause for the child, yours or mine,
who reaches across the bed at night
to hold your hand
while she talks about her dreams.

Angie Macri

The Books on the Library Shelves Looked Like Stained Glass Even Before They Burned

The fire seemed like sunset met sunrise, each flame a word
no one in the city could understand. The beams of iron and wood
joined the talk, walls jaws that opened once and never closed.
The bricks shrugged off mortar as they fell. In that noise, the books
seemed whispers of their worlds. The ashes coiled
like scrolls. The girl had loved to hold one, ruby red
with embossed gold letters that her fingers stroked,
although for the life of her, she couldn't recall a word
beyond those.
The children gathered to talk about their favorites,
one cover like the ocean, another a pine grove, the brightest
for the youngest of course, as the adults swept and argued
over the cause and cost. The girl remembered a texture like cloth,
linen her mother said once, worn bare on corners,
the red thread through the binding as if it was something
she could sew.

Angie Macri

Trailing Point

The girls bend
to play in the ditch in evening,
the sun still enough
to be hot, tongues reaching
from an open oven.
Emeralds have melted
into blades
they pick to draw
through the water,
soft but yet sharp enough to slice
a finger or palm, a cut
that feels large
though it's small. They call
to each other to look
as they take turns dropping heads
off white clovers
into the pool.
They braid the stems.
They search for luck
and, not finding it, make
their own with mud,
fixing one leaf to the three.
Why is four lucky?
one asks the other,
who shrugs. Their bodies
cast skyscrapers behind.

Ilan Mochari

The Survival Secrets of Spiders

I.

amidst anoxia felling forests, erasing orders,
you bested an era
of extinctions and sourceless scourges;

you emerged from your burrows on a fat new earth
where resinous conifers spiked the land
and hard-winged beetles munched on pointy leaves;

you spun tensile collar webs from your rear,
cylinder seals, Babel-like in their defiance,
one inch off the ground;

you mixed your shimmering filaments with dirt,
hiding behind them for safety,
and only came out at night
when your mate—or your prey—
stepped gingerly nearby,
triggering the strand your pedipalps were touching
in their quest for desired vibrations;

seeking your doorstep as pitstop and launchpad,
all those creatures landed unsuspecting;
your venom-tipped, down-stabbing fangs
bit through the mesh and dragged them, through slits, to
your silken lair;

then you restored your foyer to its original appearance.

II.

the brown recluse hides in a folded towel and bites a
homeowner in Missouri,

    marking his hairy shin with a crimson crust;

the black widow scampers through trash in Tallahassee,
    living out her years in a funnel-shaped habitat;

the desert loxoscele blends in the sands of the Escalante,
    going three months without water;

the silver argiope spins crisscrossing strands in a Miami
backyard,
    haloing a pink prickly pear;

the bola in the San Antonio suburbs lassoes a moth with her
silken sack,
    rappelling down a strand to kill it;

and the arrowshaped micrathena lays her eggs in the wet
woods of Nebraska,
    depositing them on a yellow leaf;
it's the last act of her yearlong life—she uses all the strength
in her two spines.

III.

where nursery web spiders skate scummy ponds of brown,
where wolf spiders conceal themselves amidst dried bits of
leaf and debris,
where huntsman spiders emerge from their crevices in
woodsheds at sundown,
comes a truth of truths:

it begins when a burrowing spider mother brings her egg
sac to the surface,
exposing it to the sun's warmth in the wilderness;
it begins when the sac darkens to earthy brown, till it's time
for hatching;
it begins when her two hundred spiderlings, newly released
into life, scramble onto her back;

see how they cling, leglocked to each other,
so close, so clasped — an unknowing human might ask:
is that one solitary cape
contoured precisely to the mother's rounded back?

they cling when she's meditating at the burrow's bottom,
when she's outside the burrow searching for food
in the low, parched grass of the old park with the sand-
moored swing set;
the beige blades bend like wind-whipped banners
and the mother darts between them, seeking protein-
packed insects;
and if a swaying blade swipes babes from her back,
the thrown-off babes find her anew,
her jointed legs like flagpoles in the dirt,
clung to, climbed upon, until they rejoin and re-blend with
their siblings within the fabric.

it begins where babies cover mothers with warmth,
showing hemolymph's thicker than blood,
showing shielding and coating
should be matters of instinct, not policy;
all gods and religions are leading to this,
and nothing on earth could be fitter.

Anatoly Belilovsky

The Seven Measures of Edgar Cortelyou

The Brethren of Health first took measure of him as he staggered the last league through the Wasteland toward the Chapterhouse. They charted his progress past the dry wells and the bleached skeletons until he fell to his knees at the Petitioner's Door.

Secondly, they measured his body: recorded his height and weight, and did some magic with the numbers to determine his needs. The food was plentiful and good, and he thanked them humbly as he ate. They took away the dishes, and compared the fingerprints he left on the porcelain with ones recorded on the identity card he gave them upon his entry.

Thirdly, they drew his blood and took measure of its properties. They frowned over a number which they pronounced after the word "creatinine" and before the word "kid-knees." This surprised him, as his limbs had been created at the same time as the rest of him, and were nothing like those of a child. They also whispered about "compatibility," and he promised to be as quiet and as compatible a guest as any the Brethren had ever entertained.

Fourthly, they locked him in a steel coffin for a time, and having let him out, frowned while muttering about his "liver," which made him wonder if he'd been deemed worthy of living.

Fifthly, they measured his mind, frowning throughout and muttering about a "low eye queue," and though he knew his eyes were bad, scarred by illness and accident, he wondered what was meant, as he was quite certain his eyes were at the top of his head, not low, and side by side, not one behind the other, as every queue he'd ever stood on had been structured.

The Brethren put him to work in Chapterhouse gardens. There were many Guests in the garden, some who sowed, some who pruned, some who hoed, some who raked. They set him to harvest tomatoes, their large bright fruit visible even to his poor eyes, their textures discernible even to his coarse, knotty fingers. Through the Chapterhouse windows they watched him work alongside other Guests as they pondered his fate.

"He is weak," said Brother the First. "He barely made it to the Chapterhouse."

"But he made it, after all," said Brother the Last.

"He is sick," said Brother the Second. "He stayed in the Wastelands far longer than is wise."

"But he found the way to Chapterhouse," said Brother the Last.

"He is not long for this world," said Brother the Third. "His liver, his kidneys, his intestines, his eyes, none are likely to serve much longer."

"But he has a good heart," said Brother the Last.

"That he does," said Brother the First, and everyone nodded.

And so they fed him porridge laced with a sleeping draught, and cut his chest and harvested his heart and planted it in Brother the Last who had but recently been a Guest at the Chapterhouse. They buried all the parts of him that did not measure up in a grave that measured (sixthly) six feet long, half a foot longer than he actually required, and wrote upon his headstone, "Edgar Cortelyou," in the first and last instance of his name being mentioned; and the dates of his birth and death, that his days, too, be (seventhly) measured.

ERIN SWAN

POSSESSION

In the days to come, much will fail Maimouna: the imam, the priest, her own resolve. No longer will she break into consciousness, gasping for light and air. She will no longer reach for her mother, her cracked lips parting in a *Please*. As 2007 crawls towards Halloween, the darkness will swallow her whole. Subsumed in its depths, viscous as swamp waters, she will float in a timeless suspension, communing with the pale and fleshy being that so closely resembles herself. *Shame*, it will whisper, and *Shame*, she will whisper back, unable to tear her eyes away.

In the world above, her mother will discard her sorrow, set her lips firm against her teeth and cooperate with those who seek her daughter's salvation: first the imam, and when he flees in fear, claiming not a djinn but a Christian demon, the Catholic priest. With one hand she will clench her nazar and with the other Maimouna, steeling herself against the growling, the cursing, the insults shouted by the slit-eyed creature that has invaded her child's body, until an unseen hand hurls the priest's crucifix upside down through the air, striking him between the eyes, and he too flees, and she and her daughter are left entirely alone.

On October 21st, a week and two days before the priest's flight, Maimouna chokes down two spoonfuls of her mother's chicken korma before excusing herself to complete her homework. Her mother, who still eats with her hands as though they're in Afghanistan, says nothing, but Maimouna senses her eyeing the plate she carries to the kitchen, imagines her gaze flicking from the congealing stew to

Maimouna's retreating body. Maimouna feels her hips' swell against her sweatpants, her belly's nudge over the waistband, and hurries to dump the korma down the garbage disposal. Its deep *whirr* echoes through the house. Outside, across the lonely northern fields, night has fallen.

In her room, Maimouna tackles her history homework first because it is easy. They are studying the American Revolution and war has a recognizable pattern. The last two questions require extended answers. As she bends to write her responses—*Patrick Henry sought to inspire*—a wave of weariness rises, hovers above her, then bears down. She sleeps for ten minutes, sitting up with eyes and mouth open, and when she wakes, her history textbook has been shut and slid into her backpack.

On her bed, a Victorian canopy gifted by her father when they moved upstate from the Bronx last year, rests her English anthology, open to the poem Mr. Parker has assigned. "Ozymandias." She's read it before. She's read all the poems in the musty blue book, most of them when she's woken in the middle of the night with a cry half-formed on her lips. She likes "The Charge of the Light Brigade" best (*Theirs but to do and die*) but "Ozymandias" is good too. She reads it again.

~

Their final summer in Afghanistan, in August of 2001, before the American bombs, before her grandmother's death, before they fled to her uncle in Co-op City, Maimouna's father finagled a day pass from their local Taliban chief and brought the family on an excursion to the countryside outside Kabul. In 1989 he had won a scholarship to Cambridge, where he pursued his PhD in psychology, studying human behavior and cognitive development—and the variety of teas offered at each meal. He returned to his country with a taste for crumpets and a deep appreciation for the sonnet. Though Sharia law eventually morphed his budding psychology profession into shopkeeping, his love of all things British privately persisted: starched collars, Shakespeare, croquet. He particularly loved the English countryside, which he told Maimouna abounded with babbling brooks and grassy hillsides fluttering with daisies.

But the landscape outside Kabul was neither damp nor green. Maimouna was six, too young to comprehend her motherland's terrible beauty, and the vastness surrounding their battered white Toyota Corolla muted her. Sere and brown and dry. A scrim of mountain range on the horizon. The sky so arid it had turned white.

Her father ground the car to a halt and urged them to clamber out. *We will have a picnic,* he said, unfurling a red-and-white checkered cloth in the dust. There were glass bottles of lemonade he had made himself and limp cucumber sandwiches he bemoaned for their lack of watercress, but which he nonetheless laid out painstakingly. *Sit,* he told them. *Eat and be merry.*

Maimouna remembers her family circled on that cloth: father, mother, brother. Her grandmother tilting her face towards the sun. Though her blue burqa shielded her expression, Maimouna believes she was smiling. Two months later this woman, her mother's mother, would be admitted to the hospital for cataract surgery and, while in recovery, would explode into so many pieces from an errant US missile that Maimouna's family would receive no body to bury.

~

Maimouna likes the phrase *antique land* best. She also likes *lone and level sands* stretching *far away*. Her father used to recite a Shakespearean sonnet before each meal, his Adam's apple bobbing fast on the final couplet. Gulp, gulp, she would whisper, watching his throat. She's not supposed to write in her textbooks, but Maimouna underlines both phrases in "Ozymandias" and closes the book without answering Mr. Parker's comprehension questions.

She knows what Mr. Parker will say about the poem, what the students won't. Because of her low sixth-grade scores, she was moved from Honors to General English in seventh. The air in Honors fluttered with eager hands, but in General nobody talks except the teacher. She watches Mr. Parker waving his arms like an inflatable figure outside a Kingston car dealership, straining to rouse interest in the ancient anthology, sweating in his three-piece suit. An odd fashion choice, Maimouna thinks, for a man under thirty. He told them on the first day he was twenty-five, believing perhaps his youth would interest them. But nothing interests them. Her classmates don't even disrupt the class. They don't do anything. They sit there, slack-jawed and blinking. Occasionally they fall asleep.

Ozymandias will be the same. *Don't you see?* Mr. Parker will plead. *It's about the ultimate insignificance of human endeavor.* The students will stare forward, mouths open. And though she'll want to, Maimouna won't raise her hand either. She can imagine herself nodding with Mr. Parker, saying, *Nothing we accomplish matters,* but she knows she'll slump with the rest, her eyes glazing over.

Maimouna slides her anthology into her backpack with her history textbook. She still has math and science homework, but she swore off both subjects a year ago. She wants nothing to do with reason and design, the idea the universe works according to rules. Both textbooks remain at the bottom of her school locker, where she dumped them that first week in September.

She lays out her jeans and kameez and headscarf for the morning, and goes to wash her face and brush her teeth with the neem toothpaste her mother buys cheap from an Indian store in Poughkeepsie.

Back in her room, she listens to the unmistakable sounds of *Finding Nemo* downstairs, and underneath that, the musical rise and fall of her mother keening. Then she undresses, pulls on her nightgown, switches off the light, and after an hour of restless turning, falls asleep.

At 3 a.m., she wakes on the living room floor, dressed in her school clothes, with no idea how she has gotten there.

Outside the wind is blowing through the trees, rustling the leaves. It sounds like a conversation, but without words. Their house, a two-story with beige vinyl siding, stands in a field, sparsely shielded by a few oaks, and Maimouna pictures the darkness surrounding them.

This is true countryside, her father proclaimed when he bought the house in Accord. *Look at this grass.*

She used to like the green field, but she's noticed recently how dull it looks, with none of the charming hillocks and wildflowers she's seen in her father's books about England. And now she's stranded in the house at its center, in the night's smallest hours. When she glances at her feet, she notices her sneakers are untied, though she always double knots them.

First she sits up and ties her sneakers. Then she stands and walks upstairs to her room—how she and her brother exulted over the fact of actual stairs!—and lies down, still clothed, on her bed. This time she drops instantly to sleep.

~

In the school cafeteria the next day, Maimouna requests tater tots but no burger, and eats them sitting alone at a busy table. The girls around her, lip-glossed and brightly chattering, are lunching on Diet Coke and gossip. Occasionally their eyes slide towards Maimouna, then slide away.

When she's swallowed her last tater tot, Maimouna walks to the girls' restroom, where she sticks two fingers down her throat and throws up in a stall next to a girl who, from the sound of it, has gotten her first period. As she's rinsing her mouth, the bell rings. It's time for English.

In the hallway she blacks out, but does not fall down. She regains consciousness outside Mr. Parker's room on the upper floor, still walking. It feels as though dark water has swallowed her, then spit her out. As she approaches, Mr. Parker, his skinny frame lost in his grown-up's suit, smiles at her encouragingly, but she doesn't smile back. Instead she turns around and walks down the stairs, through the cafeteria and out the door to the recreation field behind the school. She crouches between two soccer goalposts without a net, and puts her head on her knees.

When they fled Kabul for the Bronx, Maimouna's mother counseled her about what to expect in school. *You must not listen to what they say*, she said. *I am told they fear us. But remember, fear springs from ignorance. Our people are a great people.* Here she laid her palm against her daughter's cheek. *Do not forget this.*

But Maimouna had no need to worry. The Co-op City elementary school was filled with immigrants from Pakistan, Ecuador, Guyana, even a few from Afghanistan. Nobody teased her about her country or her religion or the full burqa her mother wore. She made friends, excelled in her studies, made her parents proud. When her brother grew old enough to enter elementary school, he did the same.

Even now, in Rondout Valley Middle School, no one mocks her religion. Liberals from the city are flooding the area. Their children wouldn't dream of taunting a girl for being Muslim. Islam is not the problem. It's Maimouna's body. After their move upstate, after her father's exultant purchase of a country home, after he settled into his hard-won professorship at the state college, her body began to change, swelling here, pouching there, developing bumps and ridges and folds. As she walks through the tiled hallways, wedges herself into each tight desk, she imagines her classmates' thoughts. Little words, she assumes, probably the names of animals. Pig. Cow. That kind of thing. Two weeks ago, she discovered a solution online. Use two fingers, the blogs said. Once your body becomes accustomed to two, use three.

Not every meal. She placed limitations on herself early. Once a day, no more.

Sitting between the goal posts, shivering in the thin sunshine of October 22, Maimouna squeezes her eyes shut and, when the darkness grows frightening, snaps them open. When she'd blacked out in the hallway, thick water seeming to close over her head, she'd seen something. It was pale and fleshy, not unlike her new body, and when it drifted towards her, it whispered a single word. *Shame.* That's when she began to kick upward, forced herself to break through the surface into consciousness.

Shame, she whispers to herself now, out loud in the recreation field. It doesn't sound as awful as it did in the darkness. Shame, she says again, and this time the word's power is dispelled, like a soap bubble poked by a finger. Shame, she shouts, and picks herself up and goes back inside, where she hides in the bathroom until the next bell. Keeping her head low, she walks to American History, which is her best subject, if maintaining a mere seventy-five can be called one's best.

~

In 2036, at the age of forty-one, Maimouna will recall this afternoon as a single image. A woman of strong calves and broad shoulders, she will have discarded the headscarf for a perfectly clean-shaven head, which she will carry through the Manhattan crowds as a soldier might lift a banner for war. She will be walking back from lunch to her editorial desk in midtown when the image strikes her. A twelve-year-old girl huddled on ground scuffed bare of grass, her eyes black with the seed of the thing growing within her.

Maimouna will be flooded with sadness so intense she will lean against the window of a luxury soap store for five minutes before she can stand straight again. She will realize she has not blinked, and her eyes will feel scratchy, as if she has been crying, and she will briefly squeeze them shut. On trembling legs she will force herself down Lexington to Fifty-Seventh Street, where she will turn and walk the ten paces to her office building. She will smooth her bare head with her hand, then push through the revolving door to the lobby. The din from outside will hush instantly behind her.

~

At mealtime that night, Maimouna announces she is tired of eating on the floor.

Can't we buy a table like regular people? she asks. My legs get stiff.

Growing pains, her mother says. Your body will adjust.

Maimouna gazes down at her body. Why do we have an American house if we can't have an American table? she asks.

Your father wanted this house, her mother says, but does not explain the table. Her voice quavers on the word father. Pass the naan, please.

They chew their naan and the leftover korma in silence. Maimouna has allowed herself a large helping, though it has thickened overnight into an oily paste. In Co-op City, her mother would have offered their leftovers to their Hazara neighbors, asserting that in America they must stick together, but in Accord they have no neighbors. The closest house is a double-wide trailer a mile away. Cars litter its yard, but Maimouna has seen no one on the property. For all she knows, the trailer is abandoned.

Maimouna's mother picks up a second piece of naan, puts it back down. Her eyes drift to the window, which still lacks curtains, then down to the purple cloth spread on the floor, a wedding gift.

Moer, Maimouna says, using the Pashto word for mother. She hasn't used it in months, and the word feels cottony on her tongue.

Her mother turns and studies Maimouna's plate approvingly. You've cleaned your dish, she says, pushing over the bowl of korma. Have some more.

Maimouna opens her mouth to politely refuse, but no words emerge. Instead a tremendous black cloud, thick and sooty as smoke, whooshes up her throat and out of her mouth. For an awful second, it hovers around them, filling their ears with a violent buzz, as of a thousand flies at once. Then it disappears.

Her mother clutches the nazar she wears around her neck. My daughter, she whispers.

Please excuse me, Maimouna says.

She barely makes it to the bathroom in time. She doesn't need to use two fingers, or even one. The leftover stew spews forth as the cloud did: dense, terrifying, tasting of sulfur. She flushes it, and when more pours forth, she flushes that too. She can hear her mother pounding on the door, but from a great distance. *Lone and level sands*, she thinks, *stretch far away*. She coughs once more and a fly comes out. A black one, bristly as the ones her mother used to spray to death in their Kabul home. Maimouna flushes it.

Da zra takora, her mother calls through the door, a term of endearment she used when Maimouna was young. Beat of my heart, she says, as though their existence in America calls for translations. My child, she says, you are sick. Stay home tomorrow.

Maimouna imagines her mother leaning her forehead against the flimsy wood. When she speaks again, her voice has lost its recent wobble.

I will stay home too, she tells her daughter. I will take care of you.

A week from then, on Halloween's cusp, Maimouna's mother will utter this phrase again. *Da zra takora*, she will beseech, clenching her daughter's swollen hand, staring without flinching into her yellow eyes. *Beat of my heart, come back to me.* This after the priest has fled, after darkness has encircled their house, sealing the exits, after she has realized she still has a child to save. *Da zra takora*, though the beat of her daughter's heart will sound nothing like her own.

~

At 3 a.m. on October 23, Maimouna wakes again on the living room floor. This time she is naked. For long moments she breathes, watching her dimpled belly rise and fall. She is too scared to move. The night feels as black as the water that swallowed her, as dense as the cloud that poured from her mouth. Her body floats in the darkness, a pale and fleshy mound marked by tangled patches of hair.

Anaa, she eventually whispers. But her grandmother, who Maimouna thinks could be a ghost, does not answer. She wants to say *Plaar*, for Father, or maybe *Ba-ba* like when she was little; and her brother's name, too. But she has not uttered their names in a year and to do so now, lying bare on the floor of the house her father bought for them, seems wrong.

Maybe, she thinks, if I close my eyes, I will wake up back in my bed.

She tries it and it happens. She opens her eyes to a vibrant blue sky and the oak leaves outside her windows, which have transformed from orange to violent red. Her body is clothed once more in her nightgown, though it is backward and the tag scratches her throat when she turns her head.

Moer, she calls out. I feel fine. I'm going to go to school.

On the school bus, Maimouna notices all the trees are red. No browns or yellows or oranges. Each tree—oak and maple, beech and sycamore, the weeping willows on the farms, the slender saplings by the road—now flutters with fiery leaves. She expects the other students to notice, but they're too busy listening to music or texting or staring into their own laps. Maybe they do notice, she thinks. Maybe they just don't care.

When they reach Rondout, the streak of red stops, because the trees surrounding the school have no leaves. They have dropped overnight, revealing branches black against the blue sky.

Maimouna makes it through first and second period, but at the beginning of third period gym, she doubles over as she enters the locker room.

What's wrong? a girl asks. She's blonde and thin, not somebody who would normally speak to her, but her tone is kind and her hand on Maimouna's shoulder gentle.

None of your fucking business, Maimouna hears herself saying. It exits her mouth as abruptly and uncontrollably as the vomit the night before.

The blonde girl yanks her hand back.

Oh my God, she says. You can talk.

Maimouna feels her head whip to the side. She opens her mouth to say something else—*Sorry*, perhaps—but instead a growl emerges, a deep throaty rasp that burns her throat. As its echo fades, she can smell the singe of her own flesh.

The girl steps backward.

Ms. Sedgewick? she calls. Something's wrong with Maimouna.

She knows my name? Maimouna thinks, and tries to stand up, but can't. Out of the corner of her eye, she glimpses the gym teacher rolling forward on her fat legs, her cheeks rosy with concern, and behind her a crowd of her classmates, looking nervous and afraid and excited. The blonde girl's mouth is open, and Maimouna remembers the previous week, when she saw her laughing at a boy whose pants had split when he'd bent over.

Then the dark water surges over her head, and the locker room disappears.

The darkness pours down her throat and into her ears and up her nose, and Maimouna believes she is drowning, but she isn't. She tries to call out—*Anaa!*—but can't. She pictures her grandmother on the day of their countryside excursion, her squat form swaddled in its burqa, tiny under the white sky, her gnarled hands accepting a cucumber sandwich and a tin cup of lemonade from Maimouna's father. *Plaar*, she tries to say, then *Ba-ba*, and she smells his Earl Grey scent and crisply ironed shirts, hears his voice filled with Shakespeare—*my mistress's eyes are nothing like*—but she cannot spit out the darkness in her throat to call his name.

Then she sees it. That same pale and fleshy thing, swimming towards her through the murk. It has tentacles, then arms, then legs, then nothing, an amorphous mass undulating towards her, and it is in her face and whispering. She hears static and unintelligible voices and then that word. Shame. And then it is Maimouna's own body, her despised self wavering in front of her, and she feels herself gagging and her stomach heaves and around her lifts the buzzing of flies.

~

Two years later, a day shy of the locker room incident's anniversary, Maimouna will lose her virginity to a boy five years older but four inches shorter than she. A student at Ulster County Community College, he will meet her in the Stone Ridge Library, where she goes each Saturday to read poetry by herself. He will be Muslim too, but from Bangladesh, and he will love her pale skin and her hipbones' delicate curve around what he calls her jewel, and when, with a rapid pelvic plunge, he deflowers them both, he will collapse weeping, but Maimouna will not. *Faster*, she will tell him, gritting her teeth against the pain. And later, when she examines her body in her mother's mirror, she will be pleased to see it looks nothing like how she's remembered it.

~

Maimouna is in the nurse's office, stretched flat on a green faux-leather cot. Something heavy is pressing her forehead, but when she reaches up, she finds only a damp cloth.

Feeling better? asks the nurse.

Maimouna blinks. Her eyes are crusty, as though she has been sleeping.

Right, the nurse says. You're the one who doesn't talk. Glass of water?

Maimouna nods.

The nurse leaves, a water cooler burbles, and she returns, holding a paper cup printed with daisies.

Mind if I sit? the nurse asks, and gestures at the cot. She plops herself down before Maimouna has a chance to reply, and watches as she takes a careful sip of water. When nothing happens—no vomiting, no blacking out, no horrifying words torn from her mouth without her permission—she drinks the rest in one cold gulp.

Thank you, she manages to say.

So she can speak, the nurse says to the ceiling. She turns to Maimouna. You gave your gym teacher a scare. Lily Simmons too. I don't think anybody's cursed at her before. The nurse giggles. Would've liked to see that.

She glances at Maimouna as if inviting her to laugh, too, but Maimouna doesn't laugh.

Do you want to talk about what happened?

Maimouna shakes her head.

Ms. Sedgewick and I have agreed not to tell the principal about the cursing.

Did I faint?

The nurse looks startled. No. Why?

I thought maybe I had.

You walked here on your own. Mrs. Sedgewick said she could hardly keep up.

Maimouna studies her hands. The knuckles are cracked and sore, as though she has punched something. Did I do anything else?

No, nothing else. More water?

No, thank you.

The nurse checks the clock on the wall. Bell's going to ring in a minute.

Is it lunchtime?

That just passed. It'll be sixth period. Should I call your mother instead? Have her come get you?

She works, Maimouna says, staring into her paper cup.

Her mother does not work. Her mother lives off her father's life insurance policy and what his brother sends them from Co-op City. Sometimes she shops for what passes for Afghan food or goes on long drives, through Accord, past Kerhonkson, onto any overgrown roads she can find, as though chasing her husband's idea of the country. But mostly she sits home.

Shall I try her at work?

No thanks. Maimouna touches her hairline. A few strands have snaked free. She tucks them under her headscarf. I'll go to class.

You could rest here. I could call your teachers. Tell them you're feeling under the weather.

Maimouna examines the nurse's office. Lime green walls, plastic canisters of cotton balls and gauze and Q-tips, a single window with a single black branch tapping at its pane. Shame, says the branch. Shame on you.

I think I'll go to English. Maimouna stands up. We're reading poetry.

~

Mr. Parker glances at her when she walks in, but doesn't smile. His suit is blue and his collar wide, as if he's tried to dress for the seventies, a decade before he was born.

Ode on a Grecian Urn. Page sixty-two. Mr. Parker opens his anthology. Maimouna is surprised to see it is red. Last week it was blue. Perhaps they are returning to the one from sixth grade. Perhaps this is what happens in General English: when one book fails, try an easier one.

Maimouna reaches for her bag to check her book's color, but she has no bag. She's come to school with nothing. She doesn't understand how she managed math and science. They must have done work in the book, been required to take notes. Her brain hums with static, then that swarm of voices, chattering unintelligible words. She shakes her head, and it disappears.

Maimouna? Mr. Parker is staring at her. No book today? Use mine. I have another.

He strides to the last row and plunks his anthology on her desk. It's not red after all. It's blue, as it should be. Again static blurs her thoughts. Again she shakes it away.

Page sixty-two. Mr. Parker smiles. More musings on the

infinite expanse of time, I'm afraid. It seems they thought of little else back then. A volunteer to read?

His eyes sweep the room, but half the class is already asleep.

I'll read, Maimouna says, startling herself.

Oh. Mr. Parker's eyebrows lift with surprise. All right. *Thou still unravish'd bride of quietness*, he begins.

Maimouna continues: *Thou foster-child of silence and slow time*.

As she plunges into the poem, a sense of quiet mystery enfolds her, a feeling she had the rare times her grandmother brought her to the mosque. Women's bare feet padding the marble, their burqas rustling, the high ceiling with dusty beams of light. As soothing as the sound of her father reciting four-hundred-year-old lines over steaming dishes of kebab and rice.

Halfway through the poem, at the line *Ah, happy, happy boughs*, she begins to weep. By the time she reaches *Who are these coming to sacrifice?* she cannot continue. She lays her head on her desk and cries as she now knows her mother does at home, crumpled on the couch in their empty house, her head bare and the floors unswept around her.

Her classmates let her weep. Maimouna is certain those students still awake are staring at her with their usual vacant gapes. Not even Mr. Parker comes over. He waits until she has finished, until her shoulders have stopped heaving and she has lifted her puffy face to wipe at her eyes. Then he calmly finishes the poem, raising his voice on the final two lines—*Beauty is truth, truth beauty, —that is all/Ye know on earth, and all ye need to know*—before walking to her desk, helping her from her seat, and leading her out into the hallway.

Without preamble he says, It's been a rough year for you. It is not a question. Maimouna imagines the memo sent to the faculty the previous November. *It is our regret to inform you that our student Maimouna Khan has lost.* As clipped and polite as the officers who called her mother with news of the accident. *Our regret to inform. A head-on collision. Instant death. Nothing to be done.*

Maimouna does not reply. She hasn't eaten since her mother's leftovers the night before, and she thinks longingly of the cafeteria tater tots. Her stomach growls.

Ah, says Mr. Parker. For a fleeting moment, he looks afraid.

Please call my mother. She lifts her eyes to Mr. Parker's. I want to go home.

~

On Route 209 Maimouna's mother turns right towards Stone Ridge instead of left towards Accord.

You deserve a treat, she says, and drives to Cherries for ice cream.

The leaves have dropped from the trees, littering the passing fields with splotches of crimson.

Winter comes early here, her mother observes, though they both know it arrives at the same time in Co-op City.

At Cherries, Maimouna accepts a dish of butterscotch vanilla and slouches in a booth, watching it melt, while her mother devours a chocolate sundae. She eats everything except the maraschino cherry, which she nudges towards Maimouna with her fingertip.

You look pale, she tells her daughter. Have the children been teasing you?

Maimouna shakes her head. No, she replies and realizes it is true. She plucks the maraschino cherry from the tabletop and eats it.

Is the work too hard?

No.

Maimouna tries not to look out the window, but can't

help herself. The road beyond Cherries seems innocent.
A black ribbon with yellow markings down its center.
Her mother follows her gaze, but her eyes don't dampen.
Instead, she stares back at her daughter.

It's a djinn. This thing that has taken up residence within you.

The cherry in Maimouna's gut turns heavy as a stone.
She wants to lay her head down like she did in English class
and cry, but she does not. She locks eyes with her mother.

Djinn do not lodge within us, she announces. Anaa said
they are separate beings.

Her mother picks up Maimouna's uneaten ice cream. It
has melted into a creamy soup. She tilts the cup and drinks.
When she has finished, she sets it down and wipes her lips
daintily with a paper napkin.

In America, she says, anything is possible.

School hasn't let out yet and, except for them, the
two employees, and a boxy woman in elastic-waist pants,
Cherries is empty. The day of the accident it was crowded
with students, mostly from the elementary school.
Afterwards a brief spate of counseling ensued, with talk
about what children could handle witnessing. Maimouna
was assigned her own counselor, a bony nervous woman in
her forties who seemed startled that Maimouna had been in
America almost as long as she'd lived in Afghanistan.

Let us go home, her mother says, gathering their trash.
I will contact the imam on Albany Avenue in Kingston. He
will know what to do.

~

By the time Halloween comes, her mother will believe
Maimouna is dying. *Da zra takora*, she will chant, feeling
her daughter's skin fissuring, shriveling in the wind
desiccating the house, the words of her homeland rich and
resonant in her throat. *Da zra takora*, until the carapace

around her daughter's heart cracks in two and their hearts merge, joined in a primordial pounding that has nothing to do with Catholic demons or djinns or school bullies or Route 209 or the darkness of this countryside her dead husband adored so deeply. *Da zra takora*, she will intone, picturing her son, Rafid Khan, who had liquid brown eyes, who loved toy cars and *Finding Nemo*, who died with her husband turning from the Cherries' parking lot into the path of a drunken semi driver, ice cream cones not yet melted in their hands, who had survived both the Taliban and the American bombs pounding Afghan earth only to die on American soil, a year shy of entering middle school.

Da zra takora, desperate in her throat, until two days after Halloween, at the peak of it, when her daughter's body grows so hot it burns her hands, blistering her palms until the blisters break and leak, until on November 2, the anniversary of the day the man and the boy they loved vanished from this earth, the demon hurls one last nasty name, first in English, then Latin, then Pashto, and disappears. There is a pop and a puff of smoke, as in a bad magic trick, and it is gone.

~

Their first winter in the Bronx, Maimouna's father took his family—wife, son, daughter—to Bear Mountain. They had abandoned their decrepit Toyota Corolla in Kabul, so he rented an SUV and packed thermoses of hot cocoa and peanut-butter-and-jelly sandwiches and dressed his children warmly enough so when they reached Bear Mountain, they could climb a summit to admire the view.

This is our country now, he proclaimed, his voice cracking on the word *country*. He spread his arms wide over the naked trees and barren hills. *We will call it home.*

He wanted to go to England, their mother whispered. *But your uncle was here.*

On the way back to Co-op City, a car hit them on the Palisades, knocking the SUV onto the median before barreling past it into the other lane, where it collided with a sports car, both vehicles tumbling into the woods on the far side. As they climbed, dazed and bruised, from the dented SUV, Maimouna's family heard a desperate screaming from inside the sports car, a terrible thin sound that went on and on.

I will help, Maimouna's father said, but her mother would not let him.

You cannot cross the road, she said. It was true. Cars streaked past the accident, not stopping, not slowing down. There was no way to get across the highway without being hit.

Call 911, her mother said, because that was something they had learned in their new country. On his cheap cellphone, a welcome gift from his brother, her father did.

Numbly they watched from the median, huddled together against the cold, as nobody clambered from either car. By the time the authorities—fire truck, police car, ambulance—arrived, the screaming had ceased. Both vehicles lay twisted, their occupants mashed deep in glass and plastic and metal, the only sound the cars whipping past where one lane remained open.

I should have saved them, her father said.

Look to your son. Her mother gestured to Maimouna's brother. *His forehead is bleeding.*

That night, after Thrifty took back the damaged SUV, they took the subway to the hospital to watch a nurse thread stitches into the livid cut across the otherwise smooth forehead of Rafid Khan.

He did not complain, and afterward Maimouna bought him a lollipop with her own allowance as a reward for being such a good boy.

~

In late November of 2007, Maimouna's mother takes her for ice cream again, but not to Cherries. They drive the two hours to the Bronx, to a grimy deli on Gun Hill Road that serves the most incredible soft-serve. As Maimouna licks her chocolate-vanilla swirl down to the cone, she can't help smiling, though it hurts her cheeks, still bruised from the thing that had taken her over so completely.

Moer, she says. Look at me.

Her mother glances over and nods, relieved simply to have her daughter back, but Maimouna's smile widens.

Look at how thin I have become.

As her mother watches, her eyes soft and tired, her cone dripping onto her burqa's sleeve, Maimouna stands up and stretches her lean body, now solely her own. In the weak sunshine outside the deli, bare branches clacking overhead, she could be any American girl, trembling not for the horrors that have passed, but for those that have yet to come.

KENNETH KESNER
STANDING SO UNSTILL

everyday window museum cathedral
some walk past stay untouched

now shadows slip through glass

they enter we stand back

close our eyes fall into the sun
look together leave each other

a page written for a day undone

maybe it's something to come
forget until tomorrow

trace your prayers draw your thoughts

begin where you end somewhere so far
then catch yourself in silhouette

KENNETH KESNER

MANCHURIA PARK

somehow we're drawn to a center
as an uncertain sun pulls us
back and forth between a pale sky
and gravity's broken surface

here a confucian sits in a photograph
waiting for his voice to return
he answers a long silence
by looking away

yesterday is caught in the chill
of stark branches

so will today as tomorrow

a concubine bends frozen at her waist
in a pond of late afternoon
thin ice lets her see only shadows
cuts her if she wants to touch them

white pushes back maple or birch
or some others
to hold their weight keep them still

we take refuge there and alone
not wanting to hear

LORI TOPPEL
THE NEST

Sunday morning, I open the garage door to retrieve
the trash can that has been sitting in the driveway since
Thursday. There's a turtle out there, a snapping turtle, about
fifteen inches wide and the color of mud. The head and
front half of the shell are tilted upward as the back legs
swipe at the dusty gravel and packed dirt.

It's June, egg-laying season.

Normally I'd be startled, but I was told about this turtle.
Yesterday my husband found one of our dogs, behind a row
of blooming lady's mantle, barking at her. He coaxed our
dog back into the house, but, hours later, when let out again,
the dog rediscovered the turtle by the deer fence. Instead of
digging her way out to freedom last night, the turtle began
preparing her nest early this morning, in front of the garage,
the side we happen to never use. A few feet away from her,
on our lawn, is another turtle, a sculpture made of green
stone, about the same size as she.

~

*Last week, as I was pulling out of the YMCA in New
Canaan, where I work out, I noticed police cars across the
street, barring the entrance to Waveny Park, a public nature
preserve of three hundred acres. Waveny is serene, with
historic buildings, recreational facilities, and miles of jogging
trails.*

*An accident, I thought, or a medical emergency, and I
drove on.*

*At home, checking my phone, I saw a news alert about
Jennifer Dulos, a fifty-year-old mother of five, who had
been missing since late May. She was last seen dropping her*

*children off at school, and her car was later found by Waveny.
She and her husband were in the middle of a bitter divorce
and custody battle. The children, who range from ages eight
to thirteen, were now living with Jennifer's mother in New
York City, under the protection of an armed security guard. I
remembered my twin sons at age eight, feisty, airing their joys
and frustrations to me as freely as they moved.*

~

I've been feeling down lately. Months ago, my sister's
husband of twenty-seven years left her, and she's nervous,
edged with vulnerability. More recently, a friend's husband
suddenly died, and the service was yesterday. As I walk
down the driveway to view the turtle from behind, I feel as
if the wild, with all its intractable uncertainty, has come to
me. The turtle's backside is pitched into the shallow hole and
sways from right to left. Snapping turtles can lay between
twenty-five and eighty eggs. Their rear legs guide the eggs,
the size of ping-pong balls, into the nest. I catch glimpses of
the white shells falling beneath her oscillating tail. She sees
me, too. Everyone knows to fear a snapping turtle's bite, but
I don't seem to be bothering her.

It's an honor to observe her, I think: her purpose
accompanied by such inimitable nonchalance.

When our two dogs need to go out, my husband and
I leash them up and lead them outside the gate and up the
street. On the way back into the house, we distract them
from noticing the mother at work.

~

*Soon after Jennifer's disappearance, police found blood in
the garage of her New Canaan home, as well as the husband's
DNA, mixed in with her blood, on the kitchen faucet. A
man resembling her husband and a woman resembling his
girlfriend were caught on video cameras dumping garbage
bags into trash receptacles along a thirty-mile stretch in*

Hartford. In the bags, police found Jennifer's blood on pieces of clothing and sponges.

~

Snapping turtles live in streams, ponds, and brackish water but will travel miles over land to find a proper nesting site. Raccoons, skunks, foxes, and crows prey on the eggs and hatchlings. Once the turtle has grown to maturity, it has few predators, but there's always the possibility of a car hitting the female as she crosses the road on her way to lay her eggs.

What were the chances of this turtle ending up at our house?

Within the hour, I'm excited to see her again, to note her progress, and I step outside, but she's gone. Small mounds of gravel mark where she has covered her eggs. I take four logs from the garage and place them around the nest.

Time to let the dogs out. I stand by to see what they'll do. They sniff the logs and then trot toward the woods. Our fence, our dogs, and our daily comings and goings, I expect, will help ward off any unwelcome visitors.

~

That night, flicking through channels on the TV, I learn that Jennifer's husband and his girlfriend have been arrested on charges of evidence tampering and hindering prosecution. I'm not surprised. No one is. A reaction disturbing in itself.

About a week later, both husband and girlfriend enter not guilty pleas and post bail. Police continue to dig through debris at a Hartford trash facility while divers have been dispatched to two ponds near the husband's home, the first being where he loved to water-ski.

~

I wonder if the turtle is back in a stream, river, pond, or whatever water she might claim as home. Her eggs should take between nine and eighteen weeks to hatch. Come the end of August, I begin watching for a disturbance in the driveway.

As the days pass, my desire to witness the emergence of new life grows, and as I walk by the ring of logs, I sometimes forget a woman has disappeared.

CATHERINE SUTTHOFF SLATON

Making Home

"The desire to go home that is a desire to be whole, to
know where you are . . . "
— Rebecca Solnit

Closing day on our home in the rural town of
Chimacum, Washington, comes on Bastille Day. I tell my
husband, let us storm the entry and drink to those who
prefer the smell of cow manure over car exhaust, dirt roads
over asphalt, night noise of coyote, owl, tree frogs over the
drone of two freeways, a busy avenue and noisy waterways.
No more drunks in boats singing the first line of "Are You
Lonesome Tonight" repeated like endless ellipses within
earshot of our home in Seattle.

Every day will be home-improvement. Yesterday:
wiring the new bathroom light fixture. Today: scrubbing
walls, tomorrow: new paint: Cotton Sheets in flat latex. We
make the home ours, erasing the dirt of the last owners and
leaving new fingerprints. We downsize, each trip omitting
bric-a-brac by half, furniture by one-third. Thirty-one years
of city living, thirty-one years of trying to leave.

Chimacum. Chimacum. Chimacum. The town is my
mantra, the town is my home base. He will stay in the
Seattle house and spend weekends until he retires in five
months. What to bring here and what to leave?

~

Aging is easy unless it is not. Late September, my
ninety-four-year-old mother crumbles under stenosis. She
endures three emergency room visits in one week where
she is poked, given a bedpan, asked the same questions:
From one to ten, what is your pain level? When did this

start? What medications are you on? On the third visit she is given an MRI and diagnosed with stenosis and nerve impingement in hip, in back, in neck. After one month of rehabilitation – the decision to place her in assisted-living. We box up and bring her the appurtenances of a home: dishes, clothing, toothbrush, toothpaste, soap, her wardrobe of beige pull-on trousers, white short-sleeved polo shirts, cardigan sweaters, a pair of Velcro-closing shoes, a pair of felted slippers. We fill grocery sacks with framed photos, the collection of refrigerator magnets and photos of our father they held in place, the crazy quilt from her bed, three jigsaw puzzles still wrapped in plastic, her phone, table lamps. Do we have what she needs?

My sister has placed royal blue painter's tape on every drawer and on every cupboard of my mother's new apartment. There are blue labels that read: felt marker, dinner plates, flea medication. There are blue labels that read: house keys, magazines, dog treats. We buy a better bureau that will hold her clothes and be a stand for her TV. Everything must serve a double purpose in this minute apartment.

~

In my Chimacum kitchen I jerk open kitchen cupboards, I jerk open kitchen drawers. The pasta is boiling; where have I stored the cheese grater? I cannot find a utensil in a kitchen that is half the size of our Seattle kitchen. I have lived here four months. The time it takes to memorize the grand scheme, the master kitchen storage plan is exponential to my remaining years. How can I serve my own diminishing recall? Do I need blue labels?

~

Mom—where is the whiteboard? I ask over the phone. She asks: What is a white board? I say: Look on the bed stand on the bathroom side. *Ah*, she says. She mumbles and rolls her red walker across the linoleum. She groans as she lowers herself onto the gray divan. She asks me what she's supposed to do with the board. Write my name down in the space for Saturday, I say. She asks: *Who is this?*

~

My childhood home in Houghton, Washington, sat just west of a nursing home. Residents of Lakeview Manor often wandered down the hill into our yard drawn perhaps by the sound of children, or by trees in bloom: cherry, magnolia, thundercloud plum. Our large dandelion-laden lawn contrasted with the asphalt parking lot that surrounded the nursing home. My father would help the lost into the family station wagon and drive them up the side street back to Lakeview Manor. The steep terrace between the two properties might as well have been Mount Everest given their pajamas and robes, which flopped about their wobbly legs. Branches of our backyard Italian plum tree were for eavesdropping on the fear and confusion of residents curled in their hospital beds, propped in their wheelchairs, leaning on their canes. My grandmother once asked my mother: *Promise you'll never send me there.*

I had a notion that I could find a retirement property in the country, and that Mom, a lover of tall trees, could come and live with us in the cedar and hemlock and fir and big leaf maple. I planned on time to build a small home with hip-height railings to steady her, a home that mimicked her Hansville home, but in miniature. Her stenosis revealed just how much help she needs and it revealed that I am not equipped to care for her. Was there anything in my scheme that intersected with her wishes? *No house is big enough for more than one family*, she said.

~

Moira is an eight-week-old Russian Orloff pullet whose pen mates are two turkey poults smaller than she. Months later, the turkeys dwarf Moira. Oblivious to the diminutive hen, they stumble over her. I move Moira to the chicken half of the divided pen for safety's sake. Three months later, I remove the chicken wire divider. Moira makes a bee-line to her turkeys, dodging turkey feet when necessary. Home isn't necessarily structure, but the beings that inhabit that structure.

~

When I was eighteen I packed my few belongings into cardboard boxes, drove the family's 1968 Ford Country Sedan station wagon west across Lake Washington's Evergreen Floating Bridge, and entered dorm life eight miles away at the University of Washington. I traded space and familiarity for freedom. I swapped smells of old wood, oil-based cupboard paints, and depressions in fir floors felt under socked feet. I traded five-panel farmhouse doors for steel security doors. Independence from parental supervision was a purchase worth draining my savings for. I didn't think much about home. Was it still a home if I didn't live there?

At nineteen I left Seattle for Washington State University east of the Cascade Mountains 300 miles away near the Idaho border. I craved soil and I fancied myself an agronomy student at a farm school. It wasn't homesickness for any structure that drove me back to Seattle after six weeks, it was loss of place: mountains, forest, rain, asphalt. I wanted Seattle's hills: I did not want gold and rolling wheat fields and the eternal blue sky. Everywhere beauty, nowhere comfort.

~

The little red house in the northeast corner of Seattle was the first structure to become home. Bought with a handshake and a barely affordable mortgage in 1983, when I married in 1986, it turned into a rental. Twenty-nine years later, my husband and I come to clean, repair and find new renters. Twenty-nine years later I still craved that home. We only meant to spend a month mending the house, to stabilize insufficient framing and to replace a corner of the house rotten from the neglect of a ten-year renter. Had I left something of myself there years before, like Peter Pan's shadow? I tore away 1950s pine tongue and groove, I tore away 1940s floral wallpaper, I tore away at 1930s drywall looking for that shadow. I created more work to give me more time. To feed something that was starved in me. I stayed there two years until I had enough nourishment to sustain me.

~

The euphoria has passed—that I am finally in the country. Sourwood saplings I plant today will never be grand trees in my lifetime. I renegotiate what elements of the house, of the land I have the time to redo. I clean old grit in nearly unreachable places. I work through missing my husband. His plan to be retired by now has been thwarted by a generous offer and a two-year contract. I skim-coat orange-peel wall spray to give the illusion of plastered lath. I obsess over paint chips. I make this house ours. I paint. I plan Christmas: Where will the tree go? I make a paper chain with a link for every day before his retirement. I remove one link each day.

New is uncomfortable. I find a beat up 1930's bed frame from Craigslist; I find a thrift store kitchen table. The more scratches and chipped veneer, the better. That this house is only twenty years old is a challenge but some think it is much older and that is a balm. It is a simple stuccoed-exterior house that I envision as an Irish-Georgian farmhouse. A salvage yard can supply character and the inference of age to a home with good bones. Time is a necessary element, or the perception that time has passed. I buy an old carpet—a William Morris copy—whose corners are worn from the soles of strangers' shoes.

A house needs more than familiar furnishings. A house needs stories to make it a home: A history. I can say to my

husband years from now: Remember when we drove the
road for the first time and you said our home reminded you
of a place Joni Mitchell would live? Remember when I woke
in the middle of the night to snow-illuminated field and
woods? So much snow I was snowbound for five days? To
walk to the steep slope at the end of the road, to walk back
and phone to say: I cannot come to you! Even in less than
a year there are stories: the tree that uprooted and came to
lean against the roof in the big October wind, the coyotes
that called in the middle of the night in the field in front
of the house, the fox that shrieked, the ancient maple that
crashed across the road. The fisherwoman at the Grange
who brought back salmon from Bristol Bay—a case of her
salmon cans in our cupboard now.

The sun illuminates the gouges in the pine floor left by
my mother's dog during his stay here while she recuperated.
Small stories that will drop away without notice. Oh, but
to find them years from now when prompted: the smell of
impending snow, the crack of a branch during wind, the
smell of smoked salmon as I mix it into chowder, the groove
in the woodgrain under the touch of a finger. It takes years
for a new house, a new town to become you and you, it.
How much time do we have left?

~

These belonged to my older sister, Mary Jennie, my
mother says. *Your aunt, I suppose.* A cotton cap with
yellowed tie ribbons, cotton thread crocheted booties. A
plastic rattle. A tin spoon. *What was it? Yes, dysentery.
Before I was even born.* She doesn't remember much of her
brother Leo. just fourteen when a Tulsa drunk ran a stop
sign and crumpled the Model A truck. Here is a newspaper
obituary, one quarter inch of column. Here is a certificate
of spelling achievement from middle school, here is his Boy
Scout pin. This other box holds my grandfather's effects:
eyeglasses with one cracked lens from his collapse, dirt

still wedged inside the wire rim. A death certificate dated November 23, 1965. His Oddfellows membership card. What is left of lives in cardboard boxes on a back bedroom closet shelf in a house that will be listed for sale next month. When does a house cease being a home? When do you and when do the neighbors say: *She used to live there.*

I tell my mother that she has lived in three towns that began with H: Hardtner, Houghton, Hansville. She smiles and repeats the names as if they were a nursery rhyme. Winken, Blinken and Nod. She asks me if she still has a house in Hansville. Yes, I say. I don't say that once I week I sort through cupboards and I sort through drawers, I sort through pantry shelves and I sort through desk cubbies and I sort through filing cabinets. I sort through suitcases and I sort through cardboard shoe boxes. I put items into boxes marked in black sharpie: *donate.* I put items into black plastic contractors bags marked: *garbage*, and I sort items into wood apple crates marked: *keep.*

She says, *Yes I have a house, but I haven't lived there for years.*

~

Mom wants to know where her purse is. In Hansville the brown leather bag always lived on the dining room sideboard. Here in assisted living its new home is the closet. She will fret until she finds it or it is found for her, as if there ticked something within her purse that required her attention. There is only her billfold with ID, credit card, insurance card, library card. There is her checkbook and there are her checks. There is a ledger that now lists only a weekly payment to the in-house hair salon. All her bills are paid automatically or sent to a daughter for fulfillment. She asks to see her account online once a week, once a day, twice a day, when she remembers. She wants to know how much is in savings, how much is in checking.

She'll write me a check to pay for the supplements I

bring. *Why do I take them?* she asks. I tell her they're to help with brain function. Even if we put *EFA capsule* on her to-do list, will she remember? Will they offset her inclination to eat more ice cream than broccoli, more tapioca than apples? Will they, at 94 years of age, make any difference? Should I be more concerned about calories than omega oils to grease her myelin sheath, the fatty insulation around neurons that helps us tap our fingers more quickly, smell our food, feel the angle of the ground below our feet, hear and comprehend conversation, complete the Sunday *New York Times* crossword puzzle which has not been completed in nearly ten years. To pick up a book and to finish that book. She shakes her head when I ask her if she'd like to look for a new romance novel at the library.

She puts her hand to her head, massages her head as if this circular motion will stimulate her memory, or perhaps soothe her. I lean towards her and I place my head against hers as if to try and transfer memories we have shared, what she has taught me, back to her. Or maybe I am hoping she has something to give to me. Something to help me cope with a disappearing mother.

~

If we talk about doing things she used to do, people she used to know, she cries and apologizes for crying. Is she being stoic telling us she loves where she now lives? A place she's been for six months but thinks of as living here for years. Is she depressed? Confused over changes that don't make sense to her? Does she remember the events that led her to this place? Will it ever feel like home if she cannot remember the stories that happen during her time here?

~

From my Seattle house I take boxes of books or kitchen wares or winter coats, or garden tools. I take various fluids: kerosene, fuel mixes for chain saw, antifreeze, paint thinner, drinking water. I export, I import. I stack boxes, I open boxes. I store the boxes' contents, wander the house with an item in my hand—a box of bandaids or a hand-fashioned metal heron to hang. *A Field Guide to Pacific NW Mammals* is stuffed into a box of garden tools; an auger bit with my father's leather slippers that I could not relegate to the donation box. There is a direct correlation to the length of time between my pell-mell packing methods and the level of surprise at finding these odd items. *There you are!* uttered frequently.

Sometimes I do not find a place here in our new country house for the item. Sometimes I place the item in a box for donations. I repeat *less is more* to calm myself. If Itzhak Perlman can play on three strings, I can get by with fewer books. My bones shriek when I think of what I might relinquish to the donation heap. I read on *snopes. com* that the Perlman story is a fabrication. *Less is less.* Who knows if this is the item that prompts a poem or an essay. Or even just a lovely run of words: *The black clay pot with the slick cracked top.* It is not Williams's red wheelbarrow, but it is what I do: write captions for household detritus. Accoutrements as balm for this displacement, when the euphoria of an accomplished wish has vanished.

What you hadn't reckoned on: guns in hunting season, the unending bark of kenneled dogs, the appetite of field mice in your box of garden seeds, moles in the carrot patch, holes in the fence and chickens in the sweet peas. What you hadn't planned on missing: the uncompleted patch of garden on the northeast corner of the city house, the forsythia—first bloom of spring—that wretched yellow you slashed back each March before the bud unfurled. The Chinese elm that clogged the gutters with leaves the size of a child's thumbnail. Hundreds of thousands of dirty gold leaves, chines the size of sewing thread. Down the street, the torn-down diner where he proposed. Never the sentimental one, you. Something flew up, when the walls fell down.

You miss the birds over the old neighborhood bay: the crook-necked cormorant roosting on the rotten pier, the heron standing like a statue on a pressure-washed dock. You remember the tip of her head and flip of the fish crosswise in her beak, how it slipped down her gullet. Here in Chimacum I crane my head back at the croak of the raven. One black slash and then another—negotiating through trees like actors disappearing behind a stage curtain. The next morning they have found duck eggs left as enticement. The dog barks, the birds weave through bitter cherry branches and alder canopy and are gone.

~

What does Mom have now but the ubiquitous house sparrow, the robin, the starling, the crow fishing through the dumpster. We are stunned to see a hummingbird at her next-door neighbor's feeder.

~

A morning trip to Seattle. Taking care of what needs taking care of: an aging cat's thyroid blood panel, and donations to Goodwill. At the bottom of the dirt road, I hesitate at the stop sign. A heron rises from the flooded pasture across the road, its prow of a breast bone unmistakable. A rookery somewhere? I turn down the road towards town. Above me a flock of snow geese, necks stretched like ramrods, they will be landing where the heron has just departed. They will be leaving soon for their summer home in the Arctic Tundra.

Will I come back with more from the Seattle home? Will it make a difference to how the Chimacum home feels? When we leave the city home for good, will we leave something inextricable? Something besides the notches in the pantry door that say: She was this height at this moment? Something the next residents will feel? In the end, when my husband and I are both gone, where do our belongings go? What will end up in the cardboard box labeled "keep"? Must it all be labeled for the recipient to make sense of?

Is the house anything more than a magnificent box to contain our things? What do we attach to items as we place them there? On a shelf. In the bin. Would it be a home were there nothing but us?

~

Mom's attention is on the small dog in her lap. She kisses Bobby over and over on his head telling him how worried she was while he was at the vet. All her energy on the dog. She brings him a bit of breakfast or lunch or dinner from the dining hall. She picks it off her plate and carries it back in a small plastic lunch bag that she washes and re-uses over and over. She seems most times to be living somewhere else. In her head, maybe somewhere there where memories are kept, some point in time she has locked herself in. What of fading memory? *Who is that*, she will say, when I mention a sister's name. *That is one of your daughters, Mom.* Does she know where to go in her head to find them? A room of sorts with closets and boxes full of clues? The blue cat-eye glasses, or the dishwater blonde hair among the mink brown locks of the other girls, the tall one, the short one, the one who struggled with drugs, the one so skinny you shoved her off your lap for the sit bones that poked like garden trowels. They are all in there with her. Will she come back out when she has found them?

HALEY PETCHER

A HOLY PLACE

It was a warm day in November, just after Thanksgiving, when you asked me to recite the first eighteen lines of Chaucer's *Canterbury Tales* while we sat on a hiking trail. His characters tell each other stories, hoping to pass the time and win a competition for the best story before they reach their final destination: the place where the martyr, whose blood healed maladies, died. Chaucer might have cared about social commentary, but for me the recitation was just a party trick, something I learned during a course in college. So, I told you a tale of memorizing lines while walking on a treadmill in my apartment building's gym, of my terror of making mistakes. This was, after all, a time of exploration, the beginning of our pilgrimage together.

While we walked the trail, I asked you what small things brought you joy. For me, it's still Jim Carrey in *The Truman Show* and stepping into a hot shower. I don't remember what you said. Maybe *The Hitchhiker's Guide to the Galaxy* or running marathons. You were always running.

Over the past few years, before we reconnected in a coffee shop, we had lost people and weight and pieces of who we thought we were. After our paths crossed again, we asked questions, marveled about the world, and told stories, sharing our darkest moments. *Do you know the history of Jell-O salad?* you asked. *That the cello is the closest instrument to the human voice? That running is good for depression?* You read *The Hitchhiker's Guide to the Galaxy* aloud and let me close my eyes and fall asleep.

When you taught me chess, you told me I'm a fast learner. I followed your lead. I followed your moves. I let you set our pace. You said you wanted slow, and maybe I didn't buy it, but I was happy reliving our second date, making and breaking bread and swing dancing in your empty living room.

You hummed along with any song we heard without realizing what you were doing, and though you worried it would annoy me, I thought you were a wonder. Sometimes we sang together as we drove around town. Whenever we sang "I've Just Seen a Face," I would turn to look at you, to watch each micro-expression. I knew within a second of seeing your face if you were sad or conflicted.

The last time we played chess you laughed because I could make a pilgrimage across the board and defend but never checkmate. I wanted to win but always hated that to win was to destroy. *Here, let me teach you*, you said. But the only thing I understood was that you flinched when I leaned on your knee. You told me we should take a step back, just a small step.

Do you know how it felt to be in a dissolving marriage? you asked. *What it was like when my life walked out the door?*

There are things I do not know and never wish to know—journeys no one asks to take.

I rested my hand on your knee—hesitantly, gingerly, fearing for the first time you would mind—and told you there is no expiration date for this pain. *You're right*, you said. I wanted to say, *I know*, but I remember—I think I remember—staying silent. I was a nightingale holding back a song, watching over the sick.

And maybe—*maybe* my memories are true.

Sometimes I think of the pilgrims in *The Canterbury Tales* who sought the holy martyr's final grounds in search of healing. I wonder how many have walked that tired trail.

I am no Chaucer, and this is no satirical tale. I have nothing to lose or to win.

Now—I only wish to tell you that I hope whatever holy place you were seeking brought you peace, at least in part, and that the flawed tales we spun for each other are still woven into my image of you, stained and yellowed by the sun.

Now—you are another version of yourself.

Now—you are a blurred memory, a character in one of my stories that I have probably gotten wrong.

Contributors

Christy Bailes lives in Fairfield, California. Her work has appeared or is forthcoming in *Calaveras Station Literary Journal, Penmen Review, Panoplyzine,* and *Dovecote Magazine,* and received honorable mentions twice in the Mattia International Poetry Contest. She is a former clarinetist for the United States Air Force Band of the Golden West and an MA candidate in creative writing at California State University, Sacramento. Besides writing poetry and playing music, Christy teaches water aerobics at three different aquatic centers and inspires others to lead a healthy lifestyle. In her free time, she uses running and cycling to fuel her creativity. She says, "Cycling is my favorite form of sanctuary."

Anatoly Belilovsky was born in a city that changed owners six or seven times in the last century; he was traded to the US for a shipload of grain and a defector to be named later. Having learned English from Star Trek reruns, he is now an active member of the Science Fiction and Fantasy Writers of America. He says, "I guess each sanctuary becomes by turns something to escape from. Agility is the ultimate sanctuary."

J. A. Bernstein is the author of a novel, *Rachel's Tomb* (New Issues, 2019), which won the AWP Award Series and Hackney Prizes; and a chapbook, *Desert Castles* (Southern Indiana Review, 2019), which won the Wilhelmus Prize. His stories, poems, and essays have appeared or are forthcoming in dozens of journals and anthologies, including *Shenandoah, Kenyon Review Online, Washington Square, Boston Review,* and *Chicago Quarterly*, and won the Gunyon Prize at *Crab Orchard Review*. He is an assistant professor of English in the Center for Writers at the University of Southern Mississippi and the fiction editor of *Tikkun Magazine*. J.A.'s favorite form of sanctuary is the De Soto National Forest in Mississippi, though that is currently threatened, and could well be destroyed, by the construction of the Enviva Pellet Plant in Lucedale.

Katherine Dering is the author of *Shot in the Head: a Sister's Memoir, a Brother's Struggle* (Bridgeross), a memoir. Her first poetry chapbook, *Aftermath*, was published by Finishing Line Press in 2018. Katherine serves on the executive committee of the Katonah Poetry Series and divides her writing time among poetry, a memoir, and a novel. Her poetry and essays have appeared in *Inkwell Journal, The Bedford Record Review, Northwoods Journal, Stories from the Couch,* an anthology of essays about coping with mental illness, and elsewhere. She received her MFA from Manhattanville College. She says, "I find, as I age, that if I seek sanctuary in solitude from time to time and focus on gratitude for all that I have, I can better accept the losses."

Morgan Eklund's poetry has appeared in the *North American Review, The Louisville Review, Typishly, ABZ, Whiskey Island, Anima,* and elsewhere. She is a Pushcart nominee; was a finalist for the 2013 James Hearst Poetry Prize; received the 2012 Emerging Artists Award from the Kentucky Arts Council, and won the 2008 Sarabande Books' Flo Gault Poetry Prize. She is a 2006 alumna of the Kentucky Center Governor's School for the Arts. Morgan grew up in Eastern Kentucky and called Louisville home for eight years before moving to Chicago in May 2019.

Jamie Etheridge's creative work (poetry, short fiction and creative nonfiction) has been published in *The Potomac Journal, Red River Review, Running Wild Press Anthology Vol. 4* (forthcoming), *Unblinking Eye, Wild Word Magazine* and *Wordhaus*. In Spring 2017, she won the Ink & Paint competition by the Kuwait Poets Society / Artspace for her poem, "Epithet." Another poem was a finalist for inclusion in the Goodreads January 2017 newsletter. Jamie's favorite forms of sanctuary are books and family.

Alice B. Fogel, New Hampshire poet laureate 2014-2019, recently published *A Doubtful House. Interval: Poems Based on Bach's "Goldberg Variations"* won the Nicholas Schaffner Award for Music in Literature & the 2016 New Hampshire Literary Award in Poetry. Her book *Be That Empty* was a national poetry bestseller. Alice is also the author of *Strange Terrain*, on how to appreciate poetry without necessarily "getting" it. Nominated for Best of the Web, and eleven times for the Pushcart, Alice has been awarded a fellowship from the National Endowment for the Arts. Her work has appeared in *Best American Poetry, Spillway, Hotel Amerika, The Inflectionist, DIAGRAM*, and elsewhere. She says, "We will always need to keep wildlife refuges, but I hope that one day the need for specially designated places of protection for people will only be kept in memory, history, and art."

Jenni Garber completed her MFA at Roosevelt University in Chicago. Her poetry and nonfiction have appeared at *Hobart, Unbroken Journal*, and *Sweet Lit*. She lives half her life in Tallahassee, Florida and the other half in Chicago. She says, "My favorite form of sanctuary: When I'm in my car at the start of a solo road trip and a nostalgic playlist starts, and I know a campsite awaits as my destination."

Poetry has been **Tina Johnson's** lifelong companion. So, too, has water. For thirty years she lived in Sitka, a community on Baranof Island in southeast Alaska. She returns every summer to perform the duties of a deckhand on the commercial salmon gillnetter she owns with her husband. She now lives in the Treasure Valley in southwest Idaho, where she finds rivers to be every bit as fascinating and inspirational as the ocean. She says, "I find my favorite form of sanctuary when I am alone in the quiet presence of land or water, trees, birds, sky."

Kenneth Kesner has worked abroad in various capacities with U.S. Information Service. He's held tenured lectureships with the Ministry of Foriegn Affairs and the National Chengchi University, both of the Republic of China. He then served as a Foreign Expert in the People's Republic of China, primarily in Hunan and Jiangxi Provinces. Recent or forthcoming credits include: *E·ratio Postmodern Poetry, Indefinite Space, Subterranean Blue Poetry, Taj Mahal Review,* and *The Wayfarer.* Whenever possible he volunteers to assist immigrants to the US with the enculturation process. Kenneth has always found sanctuary and inspiration in trekking alone, and plans to revisit the interesting landscape of the Myanmar-Laos border.

Kevin LeMaster lives in South Shore, Kentucky. His poems have appeared in the *Lakes, Appalachian Heritage, Praxis magazine, Rockvale Review, the Rye Whiskey Review, Silhouette, Jellyfish Review, Plainsongs, Coe Review,* and elsewhere, and he has work forthcoming in *Birmingham Arts Journal, Dragon Poet Review, Constellations,* and *Pangolin Review.* He was a finalist for the Mahogany Red Lit Prize. His work in Rubicon: *Words and art inspired by Oscar*

Wilde's De Profundis was nominated for a Pushcart prize. He says, "My favorite form of sanctuary is the escape my writing gives me. When I'm feeling stressed or otherwise conflicted, I either lose myself in a collection of someone else's, or wind the tapestry of my own poetry around me. It keeps me warm and safe."

Meara Levezow is a queer poet from Sheboygan, Wisconsin living in Brooklyn. Her work has appeared in *Bluestem Magazine, The Pomme Journal,* and *The Toho Journal.* She has worked in restaurants for over twenty years. Her favorite sanctuary is New York City.

Angie Macri is the author of *Underwater Panther* (Southeast Missouri State University) and *Fear Nothing of the Future or the Past* (Finishing Line). Her recent work appears in *Harpur Palate, Lake Effect,* and *New England Review.* An Arkansas Arts Council fellow, she lives in Hot Springs and teaches at Hendrix College. Angie's favorite form of sanctuary is the garden.

Ilan Mochari's debut novel *Zinsky the Obscure* earned favorable reviews from Publishers Weekly, Kirkus, and Booklist. His poems and short stories have been widely published, appearing or forthcoming in *McSweeney's Quarterly Concern, Juked, Solstice, Hobart, J Journal, Pamplemousse, Valparaiso Fiction Review, DASH, Tilde,* and elsewhere. His short-story manuscript was recently named a semifinalist in YesYes Books' open-reading competition. He is the recipient of a Literature Artist Fellowship grant from the Somerville Arts Council. Ilan's favorite form of sanctuary is writing a first draft by hand.

Born in Russia, **A. Molotkov** moved to the US in 1990 and switched to writing in English in 1993. His poetry collections are *The Catalog of Broken Things, Application of Shadows,* and *Synonyms for Silence.* His work has appeared in *the Kenyon Review, the Iowa Review, the Antioch Review, Hotel Amerika, Volt, Arts & Letters* and many more. His various fiction and poetry honors include an Oregon Literary Fellowship. His translation of a Chekhov story was included by Knopf in their Everyman Series. He co-edits the *Inflectionist Review.* His favorite sanctuary is art, especially narrative art in literature and film.

Alec Montalvo is a New York City poet, high school English Teacher, and guitarist of alternative rock band Good News for the Clovers. His poetry has been featured online and in print with *Cathexis Northwest Press, The Esthetic Apostle, Caesura,* and *Z Publishing's New York City's Best Emerging Poets 2019 Anthology.* When he is not writing, playing a gig, or instructing, his favorite form of sanctuary is at home playing with his three legged kitten, Caulfield.

Susan Moorhead's stories and poetry have appeared in many print and online literary journals and anthologies. A graduate of Manhattanville's MFA program, she has published a chapbook, *The Night Ghost.* She has received Pushcart nominations in fiction, nonfiction, and poetry. Susan recently finished a stint as a fiction editor with Breadcrumbs magazine. She says, "My favorite form of sanctuary is a walk by the sea or at home with a cup of tea and my cat in my lap."

Gabriel Mundo is from Highwood, Illinois and is currently a student at Carroll University in Wisconsin. In the spring of 2019, he served as Poetry Editor for *Portage Magazine.*

His most recent work can be found in *Nightjar Review, Tint Journal,* and *Up the Staircase Quarterly.* In the fall of 2019, he was selected as a finalist for the Scotti Merrill Award. His favorite form of sanctuary is his hometown. Without a doubt, his college dorm is nicer, yet he looks forward to coming home. The shower with the water pressure of a leaky faucet. The toilet handle that you have to hold down for a minute. The heater that never works in the winter but is always running in the summer. These small defects remind him of roots he never wants to forget.

Haley Petcher teaches high school English in Huntsville, Alabama. You can find her work in *Pithead Chapel, Spelk, formercactus,* and *The Cabinet of Heed.* She says, "Choosing one sanctuary is harder than it seems! I'll go with sitting in Olde Towne Coffee drinking a mug of tea."

Heather Quinn is a poet living in San Francisco who is awed by that unnamable and indestructible force that burns brighter than shame. Poetry is her prayer, and the space she inhabits to experience deep communion, even sanctuary. Her work has been published in *42 Miles Press, Prometheus Dreaming, Burning House Press, Ghost City Review, Raw Art Review, Minnesota Review* and *West Marin Review,* among others. She spends her free time mining for words that are so alive they quicken her pulse, then whispering them in her husband's ear.

Jana Rose is strength, confidence, determination, clear vision, stick-to-it-aliveness, no-nonsense, a one foot in front of the other kind of person. She is love, laughter, and kindness. And flowers. She is so many flowers. She says, "I have so many sanctuaries. My bedroom altar is a sanctuary, and when I'm traveling, a quiet church is a sanctuary. But mostly, my sanctuaries are private bathrooms, where I can rest and think and pray and touch the cold tile on the walls; and coffee shops, where I can be inspired and warmed and meet beautiful people. So many beautiful people hang out in coffee shops. They're my favorite places. "

Laura Sobbott Ross has worked as both a writing coach and a teacher for Lake County Schools in Central Florida. She was named as the inaugural poet laureate for Lake County last year. Laura's poetry has been published in many journals, including *Blackbird, Florida Review,* and *32 Poems.* She was a finalist in the *Arts & Letters* Prize and won The Southern Humanities Auburn Witness Poetry Prize. She is the author of two chapbooks and two poetry books.

Shawn Rubenfeld's fiction has appeared in the *Columbia Journal, Portland Review, Pine Hills Review,* and *REAL: Regarding Arts and Letters.* He is a PhD candidate in Creative Writing at the University of Nebraska-Lincoln, where he received the Vreeland Award for fiction and served as an editorial assistant for *Prairie Schooner.* Shawn's first novel, *The Eggplant Curse & The Warp Zone,* is forthcoming in Spring 2021 from 7.13 Books. He says, "My favorite form of sanctuary is gaming, especially retro gaming. I grew up on the stuff and I can't seem to let it go."

Anna Seidel is a German-Dutch writer living in London and New York City. She is a recent graduate in economics and philosophy at Harvard University and the University of St. Gallen, Switzerland. During high school she published a novella in German and successfully participated in short story competitions, winning the A.E. Johann Literature Prize. Her recent work has appeared in UK magazine *Brittle Star* and is forthcoming in Stanford University's literary journal *Mantis*. Her translations of German expressionist poet Else Lasker-Schueler were published in *The Anthropocene*. She says, "My favorite sanctuary, in the sense of a hideaway or place to reflect, is my grandfather's olive tree garden in Trieste, Italy. I would visit in the summer as a child and remember this was were I first started drafting short stories and poetry. His cottage was filled with books to explore: books on Japanese calligraphy and French painters, literary classics from many countries."

Catherine Sutthoff Slaton is a West Coast writer recently moved from Seattle to Chimacum, a small farming community on Washington's Olympic Peninsula. Her work has appeared in *Soundings Review* (Pushcart nominee), *Switched-On Gutenberg, Till, Hummingbird Press, Raven Chronicles, the Tupelo Quarterly,* and the King County Metro Transit's *Poetry on Buses* Series. She says, "I find sanctuary in my orchard/vegetable garden. Along with garden tools, I always being pen and paper. When I'm stuck in my writing, or feeling our of sorts, this is where I find my remedy."

Erin Swan's work has been published in various literary journals, including *Bodega Magazine, The Portland Review, Atticus Review,* and *The South Carolina Review,* and her stories have been nominated for the Pushcart Prize and Best of the Net. She holds an MFA in fiction from the New School, and has attended both the Tin House Summer Workshop and the Sewanee Writers' Conference. In her working life, Erin has spent time in publishing, taught English in Southeast Asia, and is currently teaching literature and writing in a New York City public high school. She finds her favorite form of sanctuary standing in the middle of a stream in the woods, not catching any fish.

Lori Toppel is the author of the novel *Three Children* and, most recently, co-author of the collaborative memoir *Still Here Thinking of You*. Her short fiction has appeared in *Atticus Review* and the *Antioch Review*, her nonfiction in the *Doctor T.J. Eckleburg Review* and *Del Sol Review*. Her novella, *The Word Next to the One I Want*, will be published in late 2020. In the past few years, Lori has rediscovered dancing to the Latin rhythms of her childhood, a resurfacing of joy and peace, a sanctuary.

Norman G. Walter is a poet and musician from Kentucky, currently living and working in Colorado. He teaches elementary and middle school music. He is an MFA candidate in creative writing at Eastern Kentucky University. He says, "My favorite form of sanctuary is some sort of quiet place."

Danielle Wirsansky is a photographer whose main interest is telling stories through her work. Her photography has appeared in the *Weird Reader, Genre: Urban Arts Magazine, Sad Girl Review, Anti-Heroin Chic Magazine, Bleached Butterfly Magazine,* and more. Danielle is also a playwright whose work has been performed around the world from New York City, to Viborg, Denmark, to Sligo Ireland. She is a proud member of the Dramatists Guild. She holds a BA in Theatre, a BA in English, and an MA in Modern European History. Danielle's favorite form of sanctuary is laughter. As they say, laughter is the best medicine.

Rose Maria Woodson is the author of two chapbooks, *Skin Gin* (2017), winner of the QuillsEdge Press chapbook contest, and *The Ombre Of Absence* (Dancing Girl Press), as well as the mini-chapbook *Dear Alfredo* (Pen and Anvil Press). Her poems have appeared in *Kettle Blue Review,*

Clarion, Gravel, Wicked Alice, OVS Magazine, Magnolia: A Journal of Women's Socially Engaged Literature, Volume II, Jet Fuel Review, Stirring, Muddy River Poetry Review, and the *Mojave River Review.* Her short story, "Cupcake Payne", appears in Issue 46 of the *Oyez Review.* She holds MA in Creative Writing from Northwestern University. She says, "One of my favorite sanctuaries is so old school: typing. I love to type, lose myself in the rhythm of keystrokes. Home keys rarely fail you. Even though I'm writing mostly on the computer now, I understand why Tom Hanks collects typewriters."